NATURAL DISASTER RESEARCH, PREDICTION AND MITIGATION

SOCIAL MEDIA AND DISASTERS

USES, OPTIONS, CONSIDERATIONS

NATURAL DISASTER RESEARCH, PREDICTION AND MITIGATION

Additional books in this series can be found on Nova's website under the Series tab.

Additional e-books in this series can be found on Nova's website under the E-book tab.

SOCIAL ISSUES, JUSTICE AND STATUS

Additional books in this series can be found on Nova's website under the Series tab.

Additional e-books in this series can be found on Nova's website under the E-book tab.

NATURAL DISASTER RESEARCH, PREDICTION AND MITIGATION

SOCIAL MEDIA AND DISASTERS

USES, OPTIONS, CONSIDERATIONS

TRENT F. SYKES

AND

EMMANUEL A. TRAVIS

EDITORS

Nova Science Publishers, Inc.
New York

Library of Congress Cataloging-in-Publication Data

Social media and disasters : uses, options, considerations / editors, Trent F. Sykes, Emmanuel A. Travis.
   p. cm.
 Includes index.
 ISBN 978-1-61942-461-6 (soft cover)
 1. Emergency management--United States. 2. Emergency communication systems--United States. 3. Social media. I. Sykes, Trent F. II. Travis, Emmanuel A.
 HV551.3.S63 2011
 363.34'802854678--dc23
              2011047267

Published by Nova Science Publishers, Inc. † New York

CONTENTS

PREFACE

The development of new technologies that have emerged since the mid-1990s has led to Internet-based applications known as "social media" that enables people to interact and share information through media that were non-existent or widely unavailable 15 years ago. Examples of social media include blogs, chat rooms, discussion forums, wikis, YouTube Channels, LinkedIn, Facebook, and Twitter. Social media can be accessed by computer, tablets, smart and cellular phones, and mobile phone text messaging. This new book explores how social media has been used by emergency management officials and agencies with a focus on examining the potential benefits, as well as implications, of using social media in the context of emergencies and disasters

Chapter 1- The development of new technologies that have emerged since the mid-1990s has led to Internet-based applications known as "social media" that enable people to interact and share information through media that were non-existent or widely unavailable 15 years ago. Examples of social media include blogs, chat rooms, discussion forums, wikis, YouTube Channels, LinkedIn, Facebook, and Twitter. Social media can be accessed by computer, tablets, smart and cellular phones, and mobile phone text messaging (SMS).

In the last five years social media have played an increasing role in emergencies and disasters. Social media sites rank as the fourth most popular source to access emergency information. They have been used by individuals and communities to warn others of unsafe areas or situations, inform friends and family that someone is safe, and raise funds for disaster relief. Facebook supports numerous emergency-related organizations, including Information Systems for Crisis Response and Management (ISCRAM), The Humanitarian Free and Open Source Software (FOSS) Project, as well as numerous universities with disaster-related programs.

Chapter 2- I am particularly pleased to be here today to discuss the role of social media in disasters and emergencies. Technology grows and changes rapidly. Tools that did not exist even five years ago are now primary modes of communication for millions of individuals. Of course, tools like YouTube, Facebook, Twitter and others were not created for the purpose of preparing for, responding to, or recovering from emergencies and disasters. However, our success in fulfilling our mission at FEMA is highly dependent upon our ability to communicate with the individuals, families and communities FEMA serves. For that reason, social media is extremely valuable to the work FEMA does, and they are fortunate to have partners in the social media community with them here today who see the value of using these tools to increase public safety.

In testimony today, the author would like to discuss why social media is important to the work FEAM does, what social media tools FEMA uses in order to fulfill their mission, and what the future might hold for the nexus between social media and emergency management. Those at FEMA greatly appreciate interest in this important subject.

Chapter 3- Thank you Chairman Pryor and distinguished members of the Subcommittee for the opportunity to testify today regarding the use of social media as an effective communication tool in disasters. This is a critical topic and the recent storms throughout the South have brought the use of social media during weather events to the forefront.

The Arkansas Department of Emergency Management (ADEM) has been using social media since 2008. Like others, our agency is tasked with disaster preparedness, response, and recovery of the State of Arkansas. Social media has worked as an effective communication tool for ADEM as it has enabled ADEM to capture important messages for citizens of Arkansas on sites they already use.

Chapter 4- The recent deadly storms across much of the South and Midwest – as well as the earthquake and tsunami in Japan in March – underscore the urgency of working together with government and all our partners to be ready to respond whenever disaster strikes. Social media is playing an increasingly important role in helping people prepare for and respond to emergencies, and we look forward to sharing with you today our experiences with social media in recent disasters.

As you know, the American Red Cross responds to nearly 70,000 disasters each year in communities across the United States. You will find the Red Cross there to help people in need whether they are down the street, across the country or around the world. Their work is made possible by charitable contributions generously donated by the American public and strive to be excellent stewards of our donors' dollars.

Chapter 5- Thank you for your focus on the important issue of crisis response and the central role that technology now plays in disaster relief and recovery. During the past year, tens of millions of people around the world have suffered through natural disasters such as earthquakes in Haiti, Japan, Chile, China, and New Zealand; floods in Pakistan and Australia; and forest fires in Israel. Our own citizens have faced crises, with tornadoes and floods causing terrible damage in recent weeks reminding us of the toll natural disasters have on human life. Our thoughts are with the communities that have just been hit by devastating tornadoes in Alabama and across the US.

Chapter 6- Heather Blanchard is currently co-founder of CrisisCommons, a volunteer technology community that connects people and organizations who use open data and technology to innovate crisis management and global development. Before this position, she spent seven years at the U.S. Department of Homeland Security, including Deputy Director of the Ready Campaign.

When a crisis occurs, it isn't emergency responders who are first on the scene. It's everyday people who use everyday resources like their mobile phone and social networks to share what they know. This could be a road blocked by a tree after a storm or creating a map of where they see wildfires. Today, there are many volunteers who leverage technology, like CrisisCommons, that can direct technical capacity, harness open data and collaborative tools to help first responders and communities make sense from the deluge of information that occurs in a crisis. CrisisCommons believes that information at the right time and right place can help response authorities and citizens make better decisions especially in a crisis.

Chapter 7- Have you ever thought that, for emergency alerts to be distributed as quickly as possible, they should be sent to cell phones? The Federal Communications Commission (FCC), along with the Federal Emergency Management Agency (FEMA) and the wireless industry, is working to make that possible.

Chapter 8- Unidirectional social media applications encompass a range of applications, often referred to as applets or widgets,[1] that allow users to view relevant, real-time content from predetermined sources.[2] The Department of Homeland Security (DHS or Department) intends to use unidirectional social media tools including desktop widgets, mobile apps,[3] podcasts,[4] audio and video streams,[5] Short Message Service (SMS) texting,[6] and Really Simple Syndication[7] (RSS) feeds, among others, for external relations (communications and outreach) and to disseminate timely content to the public about DHS initiatives, public safety, and other official activities and one-way notifications. These dynamic communication tools broaden the Department's ability to disseminate content and provide the public multiple channels to receive and view content. The public will continue to have the option of obtaining comparable content and services through the Department's official websites and other official means. This Privacy Impact Assessment (PIA) analyzes the Department's use of unidirectional social media applications. This PIA does not cover users sending content to the Department. Additionally, this PIA will describe the personally identifiable information (PII) and the extremely limited circumstances that the Department will have access to PII, how it will use the PII, what PII is retained and shared, and how individuals can gain access to their PII. Appendix A of this PIA will serve as a listing, to be updated periodically, of DHS unidirectional social media applications, approved by the Chief Privacy Officer, that follow the requirements and analytical understanding outlined in this PIA.[8] The unidirectional social media applications listed in Appendix A are subject to Privacy Compliance Reviews by the DHS Privacy Office.

In: Social Media and Disasters   ISBN: 978-1- 61942-461-6
Editors: T. F. Sykes and E. A. Travis   © 2012 Nova Science Publishers, Inc

Chapter 1

SOCIAL MEDIA AND DISASTERS: CURRENT USES, FUTURE OPTIONS, AND POLICY CONSIDERATIONS*

Bruce R. Lindsay

SUMMARY

The development of new technologies that have emerged since the mid-1990s has led to Internet-based applications known as "social media" that enable people to interact and share information through media that were non-existent or widely unavailable 15 years ago. Examples of social media include blogs, chat rooms, discussion forums, wikis, YouTube Channels, LinkedIn, Facebook, and Twitter. Social media can be accessed by computer, tablets, smart and cellular phones, and mobile phone text messaging (SMS).

In the last five years social media have played an increasing role in emergencies and disasters. Social media sites rank as the fourth most popular source to access emergency information. They have been used by individuals and communities to warn others of unsafe areas or situations, inform friends and family that someone is safe,

---

* This is an edited, reformatted and augmented version of a Congressional Research Service publication, CRS Report for Congress R41987, from www.crs.gov, dated September 6, 2011.

and raise funds for disaster relief. Facebook supports numerous emergency-related organizations, including Information Systems for Crisis Response and Management (ISCRAM), The Humanitarian Free and Open Source Software (FOSS) Project, as well as numerous universities with disaster-related programs.

The use of social media for emergencies and disasters may be conceptualized as two broad categories. First, social media can be used somewhat passively to disseminate information and receive user feedback via incoming messages, wall posts, and polls. To date, this is how most emergency management organizations, including the Federal Emergency Management Agency (FEMA), use social media.

A second approach involves the systematic use of social media as an emergency management tool. Systematic usage might include using the medium to conduct emergency communications and issue warnings; using social media to receive victim requests for assistance; monitoring user activities to establish situational awareness; and using uploaded images to create damage estimates, among others. Many of these applications remain speculative, while other uses are still in their infancy. Consequently, most emergency management organizations have confined their use of social media to the dissemination of information.

However, recent stories and reports describing how a wide range of international, state, and local organizations have successfully used social media during emergencies and disasters have spurred congressional interest and discussion concerning how social media might be used to improve federal response and recovery capabilities.

This report summarizes how social media have been used by emergency management officials and agencies. It also examines the potential benefits, as well as the implications, of using social media in the context of emergencies and disasters.

INTRODUCTION[1]

The term "social media" refers to Internet-based applications that enable people to communicate and share resources and information. Some examples of social media include blogs, discussion forums, chat rooms, wikis, YouTube Channels, LinkedIn, Facebook, and Twitter. Social media can be accessed by computer, smart and cellular phones, and mobile phone text messaging (SMS). The use of social media is an evolving phenomenon. During the past decade, rapid changes in communication as a result of new technologies have enabled people to interact and share information through media that were non-existent or widely unavailable as recently as 15 years ago.[2]

The use of social media has become widespread and can serve a variety of purposes. Within the last five years social media have played an increasing role in emergencies and disasters. Facebook supports numerous emergency-related organizations, including Information Systems for Crisis Response and Management (ISCRAM), and The Humanitarian Free and Open Source Software (FOSS) Project. Moreover, numerous emergency and disaster-related organizations, including universities, the private and nonprofit sectors, and state and local governments use Facebook to disseminate information, communicate with each other, and coordinate activities such as emergency planning and exercises.[3]

A 2009 study commissioned by the American Red Cross found that social media sites are the fourth most popular source to access emergency information.[4] Social media are also commonly used by individuals and communities to warn others of unsafe areas or situations, inform friends and family that someone is safe, and raise funds for disaster relief.

The use of social media for emergencies and disasters on an organizational level may be conceived of as two broad categories. First, social media can be used somewhat passively to disseminate information and receive user feedback via incoming messages, wall posts, and polls. To date, this is how most emergency management organizations, including the Federal Emergency Management Agency (FEMA), have used social media.

A second approach involves the systematic use of social media as an emergency management tool. Systematic usage might include:

- using the medium to conduct emergency communications and issue warnings;
- using social media to receive victim requests for assistance;
- monitoring user activities and postings to establish situational awareness; and
- using uploaded images to create damage estimates, among others.

Many of these applications remain speculative, while others uses remain in their infancy. Consequently, most emergency management organizations have confined their use of social media to the dissemination of information.

However, recent stories and reports describing how a wide range of international, state, and local organizations have successfully used social media during emergencies and disasters have spurred congressional interest and discussion concerning how social media might be used to improve federal response and recovery capabilities.[5]

In May 2011, the Federal Communications Commission (FCC) and FEMA announced the implementation of a Personal Localized Alerting Network known as "PLAN," (technically the Commercial Mobile Alert System, or CMAS). The FCC is expanding the emergency alert system notifications currently sent over TV and radio to include mobile phones. The government will target the alerts in the form of text-like messages to the cell phones of people who need or have requested to be notified in the event of an emergency.[6] PLAN enables government officials to target emergency alerts to specific geographic areas through cell towers, which then push the information to dedicated receivers with PLAN-enabled mobile devices.[7] Mobile devices would not be able to communicate with the network and nothing would be embedded in the phone to track which subscribers received an alert.[8]

Recent congressional and executive branch interest has centered on whether FEMA can move beyond using social media for informational purposes and apply it to improving disaster response and recovery capabilities.[9] On May 5, 2011, Craig Fugate, the FEMA Administrator, testified before the Senate Committee on Homeland Security and Governmental Affairs, Subcommittee on Disaster Recovery and Intergovernmental Affairs that he had met with representatives from Apple, Craigslist, Facebook, Google, Microsoft, and Twitter to discuss how to harness the "capabilities of the digital world to better serve the public."[10] According to Administrator Fugate, possible future applications include using smartphone-friendly mobile versions of FEMA websites to allow users to access information and request assistance, and using social media to facilitate communication between citizens, first responders, volunteer groups, the private sector, and all levels of government.

This report summarizes how social media have been used by emergency management officials and agencies, and examines the potential benefits, as well as the implications, of using social media in the context of emergencies and disasters.

Public Safety and Crisis Information

Social media have been used to disseminate a wide range of public safety information before, during, and after various incidents. Prior to an incident (or in the absence of an incident), many emergency management organizations provide citizens with preparedness and readiness information through social media. Social media are also used for community outreach and customer service purposes by soliciting feedback on public safety-related topics.

Social media also play an informational role during emergency situations. For instance, in 2009 the U.S. Army used its Twitter account to provide news and updates during the Fort Hood shootings; the American Red Cross similarly uses Facebook to issue alerts of potential disasters. However, the main source of information disseminated and sought after is generally posted by citizens, rather than emergency management agencies or organizations. For example, warning messages via the Internet during the Virginia Tech shooting in April 2007 came primarily from students and unofficial sources, and during the 2007 Southern California Wildfires, citizens sought information through social media because they felt media sources were too general or inaccurate.[11]

Notifications

Social media are also used to send out notifications of upcoming training events and exercises.[12] Notifications can also be sent to mobilize first responders. For instance, in 2008 during Hurricane Gustav, a Community Emergency Response Team (CERT) used social media to send mass e-mail notifications to team members through Facebook when its call notification system went down. The CERT group also updated status messages to notify first responders and citizens of developments as the incident unfolded.[13]

Emergency Warnings and Alerts

Although there has been much discussion of using social media to issue emergency warnings that advise citizens to seek shelter, evacuate the area, or take other protective measures, it is unclear whether social media have been used to officially issue emergency warnings.

FEMA could use social media to send alerts via status or email alerts to warn citizens of potential or imminent threats. There are some indications that using social media for emergency warnings could be successful. A study commissioned by the American Red Cross found that roughly half of the respondents would sign up for emails, text alerts, or other applications for emergency information to help them during an emergency situation.[14]

Emergency information may also help those who are ill-prepared for an incident. According to Administrator Fugate, only half of American households have emergency kits in their home, and only 40% of American households have an emergency plan in place.[15] Although not a substitute for emergency kits or plans, providing lifesaving directives and information at the onset of an incident, or during an incident, could help underprepared citizens.

Currently, FEMA does not provide social media web pages for specific emergencies or disasters. It may be argued that that having a platform for each incident would be advantageous because FEMA could provide a wide range of information relevant to the specific event including evacuation details, food, water, and shelter locations, as well as links to other cites or actual locations where citizens could find and obtain other essential needs. Social Media could also be used to provide timely response and recovery updates to keep citizens informed of developments as the incident unfolds. The same web page could later serve as an information portal for recovery, and ultimately be retained after the recovery and serve as a historical document.

Situational Awareness and Citizen Communications

Social media could be used to alert emergency managers and officials to certain situations by monitoring the flow of information from different sources during an incident. Monitoring information flows could help establish "situational awareness." Situational awareness is the ability to identify, process, and comprehend critical elements of an incident or situation. Obtaining real-time information as an incident unfolds can help officials determine where people are located, assess victim needs, and alert citizens and first responders to changing conditions and new threats. FEMA may also be able to use the information to direct certain resources to reduce damages, loss of life, or both. In some cases it might be possible to obtain this information before first responders reach the disaster area.[16]

Another potential benefit of social media cited by Fugate and others is that it may increase the public's ability to communicate with the government.[17] While current emergency communication systems have largely been centralized via one-way communication—from the agency or organizations to individuals and communities—social media could potentially alter emergency communication because information can flow in multiple directions (known as backchannel communications). One benefit of two-way communication is helping officials compile lists of the dead and injured, and contact information of victims' friends and family members.

Requests for Assistance

Both FEMA and state and local emergency managers could use social media as a supplement to "911" emergency system lines. Researchers studying the use of Twitter during the March 2011 Japanese earthquake and tsunami found that individuals with Twitter accounts "tweeted"[18] for assistance when they could not use a phone. Requests for assistance in this manner are likely to become more common. According to the study commissioned by the American Red Cross, younger people generally use social media more frequently than older segments of society.[19] They are also more likely to request help through social media, believe agencies should monitor their postings, and have high expectations that agencies will respond quickly to their requests.[20] Additionally, some studies indicate that use of social media by older adults has roughly doubled since 2009.[21] And as more older adults make use of social media, they may develop similar expectations. As a consequence, emergency managers and officials may increasingly believe they need to embrace social media technology in order to be responsive to the public's needs.

Social Media and Recovery Efforts

The use of social media for recovery purposes has generally been limited to providing preparedness and readiness information to individuals and communities. Social media could however, play a role in recovery: if FEMA adopted social media use for recovery, the agency could provide information concerning what types of individual assistance is available to individuals and households, including how to apply for assistance, announcing application deadlines and providing information and links to other agencies and organizations that provide recovery assistance, such as the American Red Cross, or Small Business Administration (SBA) disaster loans for homes and businesses.[22]

FEMA may also be able to use social media to accelerate the damage estimate process by transmitting images of damaged structures such as dams, levees, bridges, and buildings taken from cell phones.[23] For example, in Kansas a smartphone application has been used to help the Army Corps of Engineers identify and report breeches, seepage, overtoppings, and other areas of structural weakness in levees. The application allows Corps engineers to take a photo of problem area and then "geotag" its precise location. According to Corps officials, the application has helped improve the efficiency, speed, and accuracy of detecting and responding to levee failures. In addition, the application has also helped reduce human error by reducing instances of mislabeling or misreporting problems. However, Corps officials also stated the system can be overloaded when too much information is transmitted through the application.[24]

LESSONS LEARNED AND BEST PRACTICES

Scholarly studies on the use of social media for emergencies and disasters have identified a number of "lessons learned" and "best practices" when using social media for emergency management objectives. These include the need to:

- identify target audiences for the applications, such as civilians, nongovernmental organizations, volunteers, and participating governments;
- determine appropriate types of information for dissemination;
- disseminate information the public is interested in (e.g. what phase the incident is in, etc.)[25] and
- identify any negative consequences arising from the application—such as the potential spread of faulty information—and work to eliminate or reduce such consequences.

ADDITIONAL CONSIDERATIONS AND POTENTIAL POLICY IMPLICATIONS

While there may be some potential advantages to using social media for emergencies and disasters, there may also be some potential policy issues and drawbacks associated with its use.

Accurate Information

Instances of inaccurate and false information may be an inherent problem, given the nature of social media platforms and the number of people disseminating information. Studies have found that outdated, inaccurate, or false information has been disseminated via social media forums during disasters.[26] In some cases the location of the hazard or threat was inaccurately reported. In the case of the March 2011 Japanese earthquake and tsunami, tweets for assistance were "retweeted"[27] after the victims had been rescued.[28] On the other hand, some studies have concluded that information gleaned from social media is generally accurate, suggesting that reports about the spread of misinformation during incidents may have been exaggerated.[29]

Information that is false, inaccurate, or outdated could complicate situational awareness of an incident and consequently hinder or slow response efforts. Inaccurate information could also jeopardize the safety of first responders and the community. If the federal government were to adopt social media as a tool for emergency and disaster response, it might also consider doing so within a comprehensive initiative that would include adopting methods and protocols that help officials interpret incoming information and help to eliminate or reduce misinformation.

Malicious Use of Social Media During Disasters

Another concern is that some individuals or organizations might intentionally provide inaccurate information to confuse, disrupt, or otherwise thwart response efforts. Malicious use of social media during an incident could range from mischievous pranks to acts of terrorism. One tactic that has been used by terrorists involves the use of a secondary attack after an initial attack to kill and injure first responders. Social media could be used as a tool for such purposes by issuing calls for assistance to an area, or notifying officials of a false hazard or threat that requires a response. When using social media for situational awareness and response efforts, officials and first responders should be aware it could be used for malicious purposes and develop measures to mitigate those possibilities.

If malicious use of social media during emergencies and disasters becomes problematic, Congress could elect the use of civil or criminal sanctions against individuals and organizations that purposely misuse social media with misleading information.

Technological Limitations

Many residents experienced power outages lasting 48 hours or longer after Hurricane Irene. Yet many smartphones and tablets have battery lives lasting twelve hours or less depending on their use. Although social media may improve some aspects of emergency and disaster response, overreliance on the technology could be problematic under prolonged power outages. Thus emergency managers and officials might consider alternative or backup options during extended power outages, or other occurrences that could prevent the use of social media.

Administrative Cost Considerations

The cost to the federal government to launch and maintain a social media program for emergencies and disasters is unclear. The number of personnel required to monitor multiple social media sources, verify the accuracy of incoming information, and respond to and redirect incoming messages is also uncertain. In the case of feedback and polling, some may question how, and for how long, information would be compiled, stored, and used.

In addition, the federal government may experience a large volume of incoming messages from the public during a disaster. Responding to each message in a timely manner could be time consuming and might require an increase in the number of employees responding to incoming messages.

Privacy Issues[30]

Privacy concerns exist about the potential for the collection, retention, and data mining of personal information by the federal government with respect to its use of social media for disaster recovery purposes. Specifically, the use of status alerts and the creation of personal pages to establish situational awareness may raise privacy concerns.[31] Others are concerned how the information might be used. For example, would the federal government compile records after a terrorist attack to help investigate certain individuals?

The E-Government Act of 2002[32] mandates that Federal agencies conduct an assessment of the privacy impact of any substantially revised or new Information Technology System. The document that results from these mandated assessments is called a Privacy Impact Assessment (PIA). Section

208 of the E-Government Act requires federal agencies to complete PIAs prior to: (1) developing or procuring information technologies that collect, maintain, or disseminate personally identifiable information (PII); or (2) initiating, consistent with the Paperwork Reduction Act, a new collection of PII from ten or more individuals in the public.[33] The PIA uses the Fair Information Privacy Principles (FIPPs)[34] to assess and mitigate any impact on an individual's privacy. In March 2011, the Department of Homeland Security (DHS) issued a Privacy Impact Assessment for the Use of Unidirectional Social Media Applications Communications and Outreach.[35] The DHS PIA on the Use of Unidirectional Social Media Applications does not cover users sending content to the Department, but describes the personally identifiable information (PII) and the limited circumstances under which DHS will have access to PII, how it will use the PII, what PII is retained and shared, and how individuals can gain access to their PII. In 2010, DHS published a PIA on the Use of Social Networking Interactions and Applications (Communications/Outreach/Public Dialogue).[36] Neither PIA covers other social media activity such as monitoring initiatives, law enforcement and intelligence activities, and other similar operations.

CONCLUSION

Social media appear to be making inroads into emergency management for a variety of reasons. For one, accurate, reliable, and timely information is vital for public safety before, during, and after an incident. As people continue to embrace new technologies, use of social media will likely increase. Moreover, as its popularity grows, a significant number of people will likely choose social media as their main source of information. They may also increasingly expect that agencies will also use social media to meet their informational needs. Many emergency managers and agencies have already adopted the use of social media to meet this expectation. However, they also started using social media because they believe it provides another tool to disseminate important public safety information.

In addition, beyond informational purposes, the use of social media not only allows people to interact and communicate in ways that are not possible through other media, but in some cases it has allowed response organizations and victims to interact and communicate with each other when traditional media were unavailable. Some would say that social media can be used to improve emergency management capabilities and that the promise of such positive results merit further use of social media for emergencies and disasters. Others might question the administrative costs associated with social media or be concerned about the spread of misinformation or malicious or fraudulent behavior.

Assuming FEMA chooses to use social media, it is unclear what direction its form and development would take. The costs associated with social media are also unknown.[37] For many, however, the greatest concerns are the unanticipated outcomes that might result from its use. It could be argued that the positive results of social media witnessed thus far have been largely anecdotal and that the use of social media is insufficiently developed to draw reliable conclusions on the matter. By this measure, it should therefore be further examined and researched before being adopted and used for emergencies and disasters.

End Notes

[1] Rita Tehan, Information Research Specialist, Resources, Science and Industry Consulting Section, Knowledge Services Group, co-authored this section.

[2] CRS Report R41066, *Social Networking and Constituent Communications: Member Use of Twitter During a Two-Month Period in the 111th Congress*, by Matthew Eric Glassman, Jacob R. Straus, and Colleen J. Shogan, p. 1.

[3] Connie White, Linda Plotnik, and Jane Kushma, et al., "An Online Social Network for Emergency Management," *International Journal of Emergency Management*, vol. 6, no. 3/4 (2009), pp. 369-382.

[4] The American Red Cross, *Web Users Increasingly Rely on Social Media to Seek Help in a Disaster*, Press Release, Washington, DC, August 9, 2009, http://www.redcross.org/portal/site/en/menuitem.94aae335470e233f6cf911df43181aa0/?vg nextoid=6bb5a96d0a94a210VgnVCM10000089f0870aRCRD.

[5] For example see Leysia Palen, "Online Social Media in Crisis Events," *Educause Quarterly*, vol. 31, no. 3 (July-September 2008), Connie White, Linda Plotnik, and Jane Kushma, et al., "An Online Social Network for Emergency Management," *International Journal of Emergency Management*, vol. 6, no. 3/4 (2009), pp. 369-382, and Adam Acar and Yuya Muraki, *Twitter for Crisis Communication: Lessons Learned from Japan's Tsunami Disaster*, International Journal of Web Based Communities, 2011 (forthcoming), p. 5.

[6] CRS Report RL34632, *Text and Multimedia Messaging: Emerging Issues for Congress*, by Patricia Moloney Figliola and Gina Stevens.

[7] U.S. Federal Communications Commission, Personal Localized Alerting Network (PLAN), at http://www.fcc.gov/ guides/personal-localized-alerting-network-plan.

[8] Per telephone conversation on July 8, 2011, with Timothy May, Policy and Licensing Division, Public Safety and Homeland Security Bureau, Federal Communications Commission. The CMAS *Second Report and Orders* sets out the technical parameters for the carriers, at http://fjallfoss.fcc.gov/edocs_public/attachmatch/FCC-08-164A1.pdf The CMAS *Third*

Report and Order sets out the rules and regulations for carriers at http://fjallfoss.fcc.gov/edocs_public/ attachmatch/FCC-08-164A1.pdf.

[9] For example see U.S. Congress, Senate Committee on Homeland Security and Governmental Affairs, Subcommittee on Disaster Recovery and Intergovernmental Affairs, *Social Media and Disaster Communications*, 112th Cong., 1st sess., May 5, 2011.

[10] U.S. Congress, Senate Committee on Homeland Security and Governmental Affairs, Subcommittee on Disaster Recovery and Intergovernmental Affairs, *Understanding the Power of Social Media as a Communication Tool in the Aftermath of Disasters*, 112th Cong., 1st sess., May 5, 2011.

[11] Leysia Palen, "Online Social Media in Crisis Events," *Educause Quarterly*, vol. 31, no. 3 (July-September 2008).

[12] Social Media was used to organize "The Great California ShakeOut" earthquake exercise. According to the organizers, nearly 8 million people participated in the event. See http://www.shakeout.org/ for more information on the event.

[13] Status message are short messages typically consisting of one or two sentences announcing what is on a person's mind, or what they are doing at the moment. Some social media applications allow users to send notifications to subscribers when a status message is posted or updated.

[14] "Social Media in Disasters and Emergencies," *American Red Cross*, August 5, 2010, p. 6. http://www.redcross.org/ www-files/Documents/pdf/other/SocialMediaSlideDeck.pdf

[15] U.S. Congress, House Committee on Transportation and Infrastructure, *Post Katrina: What It Takes to Cut the Bureaucracy and Assure a More Rapid Response After a Catastrophic Disaster*, 111th Cong., 1st sess., July 27, 2009.

[16] For a description of how the American Red Cross uses social media for situation awareness see http://newsroom.redcross.org/2011/08/28/hurricane-irene-and-social-media/.

[17] For information and analysis on constituent use of social media, see CRS Report R41066, *Social Networking and Constituent Communications: Member Use of Twitter During a Two-Month Period in the 111th Congress*, by Matthew Eric Glassman, Jacob R. Straus, and Colleen J. Shogan. In his testimony, Administrator Fugate stated that citizenry input via social media forums can minimize communication gaps that often occur during disasters.

[18] Tweets are status messages on Twitter.

[19] "Social Media in Disasters and Disasters," *American Red Cross*, August 5, 2010, p. 15.

[20] Ibid, pp. 13, and 17-18.

[21] Mary Madden, *Older Adults and Social Media*, Pew Research Center, August 27, 2010.

[22] For further analysis on SBA disaster loans see CRS Report R41309, *The SBA Disaster Loan Program: Overview and Possible Issues for Congress*, by Bruce R. Lindsay.

[23] Connie White, Linda Plotnik, and Jane Kushma, et al., "An Online Social Network for Emergency Management," *International Journal of Emergency Management*, vol. 6, no. 3/4 (2009), pp. 369-382.

[24] "How Smartphones Are Fighting Floods," *Homeland Security Newswire*, August 2, 2011, http://www.homelandsecuritynewswire.com/how-smartphones-are-fighting-floods.

[25] Connie White and Linda Plotnick, "A Framework to Identify Best Practices: Social Media and Web 2.0 Technologies in the Emergency Domain," *International Journal of Information Systems for Crisis Response and Management*, vol. 2, no. 1 (January-March 2010), p. 40.

[26] For example, see Tim Tinker and Elaine Vaughan, *Risk and Crisis Communications: Best Practices for Government Agencies and Non-Profit Organizations*, Booz Allen Hamilton, 2010, p. 30, http://www.boozallen.com/media/file/Riskand-Crisis-Communications-Guide.pdf.

[27] Retweeting means posting someone else's tweet on their home page.

[28] Adam Acar and Yuya Muraki, *Twitter for Crisis Communication: Lessons Learned from Japan's Tsunami Disaster*, International Journal of Web Based Communities, 2011 (forthcoming), p. 5.

[29] For example, see Leysia Palen, Sarah Vieweg, and Jeannette Sutton, et al., "Crisis Informatics: Studying Crisis in a Networked World," *connectivIT Lab & the Natural Hazards Center: University of Colorado, Boulder*, p. 2.

[30] This section was authored by Gina Stevens, Legislative Attorney, American Law Division.

[31] Keim ME, Noji E., *Emergent use of social media: a new age of opportunity for disaster resilience*, Am J Disaster Med. 2011 Jan-Feb;6(1):47-54.

[32] 44 U.S.C. 36.

[33] Section 208 (b)(1)(A)(ii) of the E-Government Act requires a privacy impact assessment for the collection of PII from ten or more individuals other than agencies, instrumentalities, or employees of the United States. Federal agencies must obtain OMB approval and publish a notice in the Federal Register to conduct such a collection. In addition, under Section (e)(3) of the Privacy Act, when an individual is asked to supply information, notice is required on the form or on a separate form that can be retained by the individual. Privacy Act of 1974, 5 U.S.C. § 552a(e)(3). The Privacy Act of 1974 (5 U.S.C. sec. 552) imposes certain requirements on federal agencies with respect to personal information maintained within a system of records, and requires the federal government to publish notice of the systems of records creation in the Federal Register.

[34] The Fair Information Privacy Principles governing the use of personally identifiable information (PII) are: Transparency, Individual Participation, Purpose Specification, Data Minimization, Use Limitation, Data Quality and Integrity, Security, and Accountability and Auditing, http://www.dhs.gov/xlibrary/assets/privacy/ privacy_policyguide_2008-01.pdf.

[35] http://www.dhs.gov/xlibrary/assets/privacy/privacy_pia_dhswide_unidirectionalsocial media. pdf

[36] http://www.dhs.gov/xlibrary/assets/privacy/privacy_pia_dhs_socialnetworkinginteractions.pdf

[37] For further analysis of funding emergency communications see CRS Report R41842, *Funding Emergency Communications: Technology and Policy Considerations*, by Linda K. Moore.

In: Social Media and Disasters   ISBN: 978-1- 61942-461-6
Editors: T. F. Sykes and E. A. Travis   © 2012 Nova Science Publishers, Inc

Chapter 2

STATEMENT OF CRAIG FUGATE, ADMINISTRATOR, FEDERAL EMERGENCY MANAGEMENT AGENCY, BEFORE THE SENATE COMMITTEE ON HOMELAND SECURITY AND GOVERNMENTAL AFFAIRS. HEARING ON "UNDERSTANDING THE POWER OF SOCIAL MEDIA AS A COMMUNICATION TOOL IN THE AFTERMATH OF DISASTERS" [*]

I. INTRODUCTION

Good morning Chairman Pryor and distinguished Members of the Subcommittee. My name is Craig Fugate, and I am the Administrator of the Federal Emergency Management Agency (FEMA). It is an honor to appear before you today on behalf of FEMA and the Department of Homeland Security.

---

[*] This is an edited, reformatted and augmented version of statement given by Craig Fugate, Administrator Federal Emergency Management Agency, Understanding the Power of Social Media as a Communication Tool in the Aftermath of Disasters, before the Senate Committee on Homeland Security and Governmental Affairs, Subcommittee on Disaster Recovery and Intergovernmental Affairs, Washington, DC, on May 5, 2011.

I am particularly pleased to be here today to discuss the role of social media in disasters and emergencies. Technology grows and changes rapidly. Tools that did not exist even five years ago are now primary modes of communication for millions of individuals. Of course, tools like YouTube, Facebook, Twitter and others were not created for the purpose of preparing for, responding to, or recovering from emergencies and disasters. However, our success in fulfilling our mission at FEMA is highly dependent upon our ability to communicate with the individuals, families and communities we serve. For that reason, social media is extremely valuable to the work we do, and we are fortunate to have partners in the social media community with us here today who see the value of using these tools to increase public safety.

In my testimony today, I would like to discuss why social media is important to the work we do, what social media tools FEMA uses in order to fulfill our mission, and what the future might hold for the nexus between social media and emergency management. We at FEMA greatly appreciate your interest in this important subject.

II. The Importance of Social Media in Emergency Management

FEMA's "Whole Community" approach to emergency management recognizes that individuals, families and communities are our greatest assets and the keys to our success. In order to fulfill our mission, we must recognize that the public is an important participant in the emergency management community and that we must work together as one team. The notion of treating the public as a resource rather than a liability is at the heart of our emergency management framework.

Communication in and around a disaster is a critical, life-saving part of FEMA's mission. Social media provides the tools needed to minimize the communication gap and participate effectively in an active, ongoing dialogue. Social media is an important part of the "Whole Community" approach because it helps to facilitate the vital two-way communication between emergency management agencies and the public, and it allows us to quickly and specifically share information with state and local governments as well as the public.

However, it is just as important that these parties be able to share information with us. I often say that individuals, families and communities are our nation's 'first' first responders. The sooner we are able to ascertain the on-the-ground reality of a situation, the better we will be able to coordinate our response effort in support of our citizens and first responders. Through the use of social media, we can disseminate important information to individuals and communities, while also receiving essential real-time updates from those with first-hand awareness.

Most importantly, social media is imperative to emergency management because the public uses these communication tools regularly. Rather than trying to convince the public to adjust to the way we at FEMA communicate, we must adapt to the way the public communicates by leveraging the tools that people use on a daily basis. We must use social media tools to more fully engage the public as a critical partner in our efforts.

III. FEMA's Social Media Tools

FEMA uses multiple social media technologies to reach the public where they already go for information and provide valuable disaster and preparedness information. Social media platforms are valuable tools in our toolbox. While no individual tool is exhaustive or all-encompassing, each allows us to communicate with the populations we serve – before, during and after a disaster occurs. I would like to discuss a few of the social media tools we use at FEMA, and how we use them.

Official FEMA Channels on Third Party Sites

FEMA utilizes the resources of several non-governmental social media channels – such as YouTube, Facebook and Twitter – as tools to communicate with the public. On FEMA's Facebook page, our more than 33,000 followers can receive updates on current situations and get preparedness tips through text, photos and videos. We also post information in Spanish.

On FEMA's YouTube page, users can watch videos detailing FEMA's response and recovery efforts, along with clips on topics such as how to prepare a disaster kit, what to do and where to go in an emergency, and how to apply for disaster assistance. The same videos are available on www.fema.gov.

FEMA's Twitter account offers brief updates to those looking for disaster preparedness or situational updates, including tweets in Spanish. FEMA also uses sixteen different Twitter accounts, including:

- A main FEMA account (@fema);
- My account, which I update regularly (@CraigatFEMA);
- The Ready Campaign account, designed to educate and empower Americans to prepare for and respond to emergencies (@ReadydotGov);
- Citizen Corps, which helps coordinate volunteer activities that will make our communities safer, stronger, and better prepared to respond to any emergency situation (@citizen_corps);
- U.S. Fire Administration, which provides national leadership to foster a solid foundation for our fire and emergency services stakeholders in prevention, preparedness, and response (@usfire);
- The Louisiana Recovery Office, servicing Louisiana communities recovering from Hurricanes Katrina and Rita (@femaLRO);
- Each FEMA regional office also posts on its own Twitter account, providing localized information on FEMA activities.

Twitter users can also follow topics of conversation that are of interest to them by following a "hashtag," which is the name given to a common topic of conversation on Twitter. The Social Media in Emergency Management hashtag (#smem), while not created by FEMA, allows all members of the emergency management community to connect and talk, including emergency managers at the federal, state and local levels, technology volunteers, private sector entities and interested individuals. I am an active participant in the #smem conversation.

In order to facilitate further discussion, FEMA created the #imprepared and #kidsfiresafety hashtags, and in partnership with the American Red Cross, created the #howihelp hashtag. The #imprepared hashtag is used to encourage individuals and families to get prepared; the #kidsfiresafety hashtag is used to encourage parents to practice fire safety tips; and the #howihelp hashtag is used to encourage people to talk about how they help their neighbors and communities.

While YouTube, Facebook and Twitter have different capabilities and audiences, we use each of these tools as a way to facilitate two-way dialogue with the communities we serve.

Finally, last year, FEMA signed an agreement with Google Books to make FEMA publications available in a free, online format. Many FEMA publications are also be available through Google Books to e-readers, allowing the public to read FEMA publications in a portable format. We continue to look for new ways to use technology and social media to eliminate barriers to communication between FEMA and the public.

www.Challenge.gov

One of the ways we treat the public as an emergency management resource is through www.challenge.gov, the federal government's platform for soliciting public input for creative solutions to government challenges. Between October 2010 and January 29, 2011, we accepted ideas for innovative and effective ways communities can prepare for a disaster before it strikes. We posted over 150 submissions from the public, and will promote the winning idea on the FEMA website in the coming weeks. Individuals and state and local governments can also view the submissions, providing one more mechanism for sharing ideas and best practices across the emergency management community.

FEMA's Presence on the Internet

The FEMA homepage is frequently updated to provide the most relevant and up-to-date information to the public, prominently displaying preparedness information, links for disaster assistance, and updates on any ongoing situations.

In December 2010, FEMA also created a blog (www.blog.fema.gov), which provides information before, during and after a disaster strikes, and highlights the best practices, innovative ideas and insights that are being used across the emergency management community.

Ready is FEMA's personal preparedness campaign. Through its website, www.ready.gov, Ready is designed to educate and empower Americans to prepare for and respond to all emergencies, including natural disasters and potential terrorist attacks. The goal of the campaign is to get the public involved and ultimately to increase the level of basic preparedness across the nation.

FEMA's Mobile Website

In early 2010, FEMA launched its first-ever mobile website, which allows the public to view our easy to load web pages directly on their smartphones. The mobile site features information on what to do before, during and after a disaster, along with the ability to apply for federal disaster assistance directly from your phone. As we witnessed during the response to the Georgia and Tennessee floods in 2009 and 2010, disaster survivors often have little with them but their phones. As a result, providing the ability to register for assistance from smartphones enables us to immediately mobilize the appropriate assistance to support our citizens' needs during disasters.

IV. WHAT'S NEXT FOR SOCIAL MEDIA IN DISASTERS

While we have greatly improved our ability to communicate with the communities we serve by tapping into new technology and social media, we cannot stop there. Over the past two years, I have met with representatives from Apple, Craigstlist, Facebook, Google, Microsoft and Twitter to continue the discussion on how we can harness the ever-changing capabilities of the digital world to better serve the public. While we have come a long way, we must continue to change and evolve the way we do business. We can do this in several ways.

Plan for Mobile

Cell phones are data centers, capable of quickly accessing and storing a large amount of information. Cell phones are continually gaining new capabilities, providing internet access, the latest weather, and access to our favorite social networking sites. For these reasons, cell phones are a lifeline during and after an emergency.

One of the major lessons we learned from the January 2010 earthquake in Haiti was that even if the physical infrastructure of an area is completely destroyed, the cellular infrastructure may be able to bounce back quickly, allowing emergency managers to relay important disaster-related information and enabling the public to request help from local first responders.

The fact that individuals are likely to have their cell phones on them in a disaster environment is highly relevant to how we must plan for disasters.

FEMA's mobile site is an important step in the right direction, and I encourage my state and local counterparts to create mobile versions of their websites that are easy to navigate from smartphones, allowing the public to receive localized information during a disaster. In particular, we learned that text messaging was a key communication stream during Haiti. Survivors were even sending information on their locations via text – this proved helpful for everything from search and rescue to commodities distribution centers.

State and Local Participation in Social Media

We also continue to encourage state and local governments to engage with the public via social networking sites. Many states and localities are already taking action, and we are happy to support those efforts. For example, in the aftermath of the 2009 flooding in Tennessee, we worked with the Tennessee Emergency Management Agency (TEMA) and set up a joint Facebook page that we used as a resource to provide the public with the latest information about ongoing disaster response and recovery efforts in Tennessee. Now that the main recovery phase has concluded, TEMA uses the Facebook page as its own means to share preparedness and disaster-related information.

Receiving Valuable Input from the Public

We value two-way communication not only because it allows us to send important disaster-related information to the people who need it, but also because it allows us to incorporate critical updates from the individuals who experience the on-the-ground reality of a disaster. The exigent nature of emergency management makes time a critical resource. The sooner we are able to comprehend the full scope of the disaster, the better able we are to support our citizens and first responders. For that reason, we must seek out and incorporate information provided by the public.

This means that we must incorporate relevant information from all sources – including government at all levels, volunteer groups, the private sector, and also the public – in order to produce what we call a common operating picture. We must integrate public input and move away from a government-centric approach to emergency management. I have challenged my governmental and private sector partners to "free the data" by making non-sensitive disaster-related information like evacuation routes and shelter locations available and accessible to the public, so we can share the best information we have for decision-making in disasters. FEMA also looks at how we can view this information geospatially by plotting it onto a map, in order to improve our situational awareness during and after a catastrophic event.

A New Kind of Personal Preparedness

I have often said that a commitment to personal preparedness among the individuals, families and communities we serve is one of the most important keys to our success. Traditionally, that has meant doing things like having an emergency kit and a plan to reunite with one's family, and that remains important. However, cell phones and social media have created new ways in which individuals can prepare themselves for disasters. A family or personal communication plan for disasters might include the following:

- Store useful phone numbers in your phone, including local police, fire departments and your utility company;
- Create a group for your emergency contacts on your cell phone;
- Know what social media tools are available to you at the state and local level, so that you can quickly access them in the event of an emergency;
- Have an extra battery for your phone (or a solar charger) in your emergency kit;
- In the aftermath of a disaster, update your social media channels to let your friends and family know you are safe by simply saying "I'm OK." This helps reduce the volume of phone calls in an area so that necessary communications can continue to be made.

Personal and family preparedness is extremely important regardless of the disaster. However, as technology grows and changes, so will the ways in which individuals and families must prepare for disasters.

CONCLUSION

At the heart of all of our preparedness, response and recovery efforts is our strong belief that as members of a community, we bear the responsibility for ensuring the well-being of those around us when a situation demands collective action. Similarly, being able to rely on one another for help in a crisis makes our communities closer and stronger. It is that interdependence that makes two-way communication in a disaster so important.

My pledge to the individuals and communities we serve is that rather than asking them to change the way they communicate to fit our system, we will continue to change the way we do business to fit the way they communicate. In doing so, we will not only reach the largest possible audience to share important information, but we will help facilitate a two-way communication, engaging the individuals, families and communities as a critical part of our emergency management team.

Thank you again for the opportunity to appear before you today. I am happy to answer any questions the Subcommittee may have.

In: Social Media and Disasters　　　　　ISBN: 978-1- 61942-461-6
Editors: T. F. Sykes and E. A. Travis　　© 2012 Nova Science Publishers, Inc

Chapter 3

TESTIMONY OF RENEE PRESLAR, DEPUTY PUBLIC INFORMATION OFFICER, ARKANSAS DEPARTMENT OF EMERGENCY MANAGEMENT, BEFORE THE SENATE COMMITTEE ON HOMELAND SECURITY AND GOVERNMENTAL AFFAIRS. HEARING ON "UNDERSTANDING THE POWER OF SOCIAL MEDIA AS A COMMUNICATION TOOL IN THE AFTERMATH OF DISASTERS"[*]

INTRODUCTION

Thank you Chairman Pryor and distinguished members of the Subcommittee for the opportunity to testify today regarding the use of social media as an effective communication tool in disasters. This is a critical topic and the recent storms throughout the South have brought the use of social media during weather events to the forefront.

---

[*] This is an edited, reformatted and augmented version of testimony given by Ms. Renee Preslar, Deputy Public Information Officer, Arkansas Department of Emergency Management, TESTIMONY Before the Senate Homeland Security and Governmental Affairs Committee, Subcommittee on Disaster Recovery and Intergovernmental Affairs, Understanding the Power of Social Media as a Communications Tool in the Aftermath of Disasters on May 5, 2011.

The Arkansas Department of Emergency Management (ADEM) has been using social media since 2008. Like others, our agency is tasked with disaster preparedness, response, and recovery of the State of Arkansas. Social media has worked as an effective communication tool for ADEM as it has enabled ADEM to capture important messages for citizens of Arkansas on sites they already use.

ADEM began with Facebook, primarily as a preparedness tool, using it to educate Arkansans on disaster preparedness. ADEM then expanded its audience by utilizing YouTube. In the fall of 2008, a personal Twitter account was created by an ADEM's Public Relations employee. The Twitter account was created to determine whether Twitter could be a social site for ADEM to consider. During the ice storm of 2009, it was noted that the public used Twitter, among other social platforms, to obtain disaster related information. Information on the site gave the public road openings/closings, shelter location/availability, and energy outages. At that time, it was determined ADEM should have a presence on the site and similar sites.

It was determined Arkansans were utilizing social sites and would benefit from information that ADEM was sharing with media outlets. ADEM expanded to Twitter in 2009 with the Mena tornadoes and utilized the social media tools for communication. With the use of the social sites it became easier to get essential information to citizens. Rumor control became easier now that we had established a presence on the sites and the public would refer rumors to ADEM for validation. ADEM used social sites to communicate directly with disaster impacted citizens, families of impacted citizens, reporters, and volunteer organizations. Media outlets began retweeting ADEM's messages which allowed for an even larger audience to be reached. ADEM noticed the social media's full potential as a crisis communications tool.

Those in the emergency management field often say that a nation, state, and community are only as prepared as its citizens; and it is true. Social media has enabled the state and local emergency management agencies to prepare their communities by bringing preparedness information to them.

ADEM encourages local Offices of Emergency Management (OEMs) to engage in tools their communities are using. When time and resources are limited, emergency managers need make use of primarily tools that their audiences employ. Of the citizens that utilize social sites, the majority are found on Facebook and some on Twitter. Social sites have given local emergency managers a site to post disaster related information and interact with their communities without website development knowledge required.

PREPAREDNESS

Arkansas uses social media as a tool to make preparedness information available to citizens. Examples of ADEM messages include, tips on preparing for disaster, scheduled preparedness events, and training opportunities. Creation and communication of preparedness messages before a disaster is significant. Creation during a disaster only assists in the preparedness for the next one.

ADEM also uses the Facebook page as an opportunity to illustrate to Arkansans that state agencies collaborate by sharing information sister agencies, local emergency management offices, as well as other states' emergency management agencies.

In a disaster, the question is always asked, "What did you do in advance to prepare Arkansans for this?" Using social sites is one way ADEM educates individuals on the importance of self preparation.

During National Preparedness Month 2010, ADEM and the Arkansas Chapter of the American Red Cross teamed up on Facebook and Twitter to issue daily messages on preparedness. This partnership enabled delivery of messages to Arkansans in a medium that allows citizens to respond with questions and/or comments, as well as share disaster related information with others.

Local OEMs make use of social platforms in the same fashion as state agencies. Social media sites, such as Facebook, assist local OEMS in locating citizens who offer their assistance in disasters.

Social media sites help communities stay involved with local emergency management. A Facebook page allows communities to understand the extent local OEMs go to in order to keep their communities prepared. Rural areas may not have much as far as media is concerned and some local governments have limited resources for a website. If one exists, it may just list basic contact information. Having a virtual location where the county emergency management office can post what is going on in their community; the steps it takes for them to be prepared; the actions that they take during a disaster; and places the community can go to get trained...it all is involvement. When the time comes that a citizen needs help they are going to know where to get it. And if they specifically are not on these sites to see this information, chances are someone they know is.

Lastly, we use it for preparedness because social media gives us an opportunity to directly communicate with our audience. While we still use traditional media outlets; it is no longer our only option. If questions or rumors come up, we can not only go to media outlets to help answer and correct, we can also answer them directly.

RESPONSE

Social media has become a huge asset during the response phase of disasters. It provides the capability of putting information out as we get it. Often in response, by the time public affairs has gathered information, written a release, and received approval to distribute, the message released is not the newest information available. Incorporating social media into our communications plan allows us to keep the public up-to-date as information is available.

Like in preparedness, this does not mean we stop traditional media and press releases; it just means we now have an ability to stay on top of the audiences' expectations. ADEM tries to develop and issue an initial statement within 15 minutes of being made aware of a situation. Social platforms allow us to not only reach the media within that time frame, but reach Arkansans directly. Having a constant flow of information in short bursts lets citizens know the State is working. Responding within 15 minutes of an incident saying, "ADEM is monitoring the XXXX and is ready to assist counties with whatever resources are needed" is enough in the beginning for Arkansans to see the State is doing something. Would we write a press release with one sentence? No, but it is acceptable to write a one sentence message on social sites. As the situation continues, it allows the public to receive information as it happens.

ADEM uses its social sites during the disaster response phase: keeping Arkansans up-to-date on weather watches and warnings (at least the information on where to find the alerts); reporting areas with damage; assisting locals in evacuation notices, rumor control; monitoring what is going on across the state; answering individual questions from citizens.

Online it is important for everything to be linked together to create order. Having data available is great, but until we know what to do with the data and until our audience is able to put data together, it does not become a usable message. Making our data searchable is a great way to ensure that when our audience is looking for information, they will find it.

One way ADEM has created order in monitoring Twitter is by setting pre-established hashtags. In January of 2010 we polled our followers on Twitter and asked what hashtag they would like to see for the upcoming winter weather – we wanted to establish something in advance to have some order to the data we monitored. As suggestions came, we realized we could create one hashtag for all weather related events. In doing so we could narrow our monitoring responsibilities down considerably. Instead of attempting to track everything anyone in the state of Arkansas was posting as individual events, tornadoes, ice storms, floods, severe weather, drought, we could follow it all by using one designated hashtag. After all, we did not want all the data that was out there, only what was relevant to Arkansas weather. #ARwx was created for the simplicity of working for all weather events in the state of Arkansas. It also happened to be only a few characters long so most messages aren't affected by its presence.

We involved our followers in the creation of our hashtag for one reason. Social media is all about community involvement. In order for our hashtag to be a success it had to be used. A large part of the #ARwx success is due to the fact that ADEM did not push a hashtag on anyone, but instead went in the direction the Arkansans wanted. Once #ARwx was created we publicized it. Messages were sent out before potential weather events reminding people to use it.

Meteorologists also joined, as well as storm trackers from all over the state. Currently it stands as a valued resource for Arkansas weather information. Not only has it gained the attention and use of current Arkansas twitter users, but also national media outlets looking for our state's severe weather information through twitter. We are also aware of citizens who have created twitter accounts for the sole purpose of following #ARwx in severe weather. In seeing how well the public responded, we also established a hashtag for earthquake information, #AReq.

Currently a gap exists in Arkansas with the ability to push information to multiple sites without having someone physically push a button, or multiple buttons. Social media is currently housed in public affairs and while one of us is on-call at all times, the sites are not monitored 24/7. If alerts come out in the middle of the night, they do not get posted. To make up for this we have made it known that while we post some weather alerts, our social sites should not be anyone's single source of information for severe weather alerts. We direct people to the National Weather Service since they are the ones who issue the watches and warnings.

We are aware of the forthcoming Integrated Public Alert and Warning System (IPAWS) which is supposed to make it easier to issue warnings to citizens. Arkansas has elected to be a part of the pilot to test its abilities.

RECOVERY

Social media tools are useful in assisting in the recovery phase because they are able to bring the community together. Again, these sites enable us to talk with each other instead of to each other. Information about aid is able to be disbursed and then shared by anyone that wants to pass along the information. As individuals have questions they are able to direct them to us in a familiar format. We also post pictures of damaged areas to reinforce preparedness.

At this time the only privacy concerns I can see would be if someone was to discuss their assistance applications on a social site, asking ADEM for input. Assistance applications are not discussed through social sites. If a citizen was to initiate the conversation concerning their application the State's response would be to ensure the individual that they would be personally contacted regarding the status. Details are not to be discussed socially.

BARRIERS

The largest barrier was broken when our federal family began engaging in social sites. Before then, it was difficult for states and locals to say they were going to do something, or that it was acceptable to do something that the federal government had not yet adopted.

I believe that the federal government can work with social media companies to create a uniform analytics application for emergency managers to use. This would help emergency personnel see what messages were being received and which messages should need to be approached differently.

CONCLUSION

Thank you for the opportunity to provide testimony today and I look forward to any questions the Subcommittee members may have.

In: Social Media and Disasters   ISBN: 978-1- 61942-461-6
Editors: T. F. Sykes and E. A. Travis   © 2012 Nova Science Publishers, Inc

Chapter 4

TESTIMONY OF SUZY DEFRANCIS, CHIEF PUBLIC AFFAIRS OFFICER, AMERICAN RED CROSS, BEFORE THE SENATE COMMITTEE ON HOMELAND SECURITY AND GOVERNMENTAL AFFAIRS. HEARING ON "UNDERSTANDING THE POWER OF SOCIAL MEDIA AS A COMMUNICATION TOOL IN THE AFTERMATH OF DISASTERS" *

Good afternoon Mr. Chairman, Members and staff of the Subcommittee. This is a very timely gathering to address an extremely important subject, and we appreciate the opportunity to provide our perspective.

The recent deadly storms across much of the South and Midwest – as well as the earthquake and tsunami in Japan in March – underscore the urgency of working together with government and all our partners to be ready to respond whenever disaster strikes. Social media is playing an increasingly important

---

* This is an edited, reformatted and augmented version of testimony given by Suzy Defrancis, Chief Public Affairs Officer, American Red Cross, before the U.S. Senate Homeland Security & Governmental Affairs Committee, Subcommittee on Disaster Recovery & Intergovernmental Affairs, Understanding the Power of Social Media as a Communication Tool as We Prepare for and Respond to Disasters, on May 5, 2011.

role in helping people prepare for and respond to emergencies, and we look forward to sharing with you today our experiences with social media in recent disasters.

As you know, the American Red Cross responds to nearly 70,000 disasters each year in communities across the United States. You will find the Red Cross there to help people in need whether they are down the street, across the country or around the world. Our work is made possible by charitable contributions generously donated by the American public, and we strive to be excellent stewards of our donors' dollars.

AMERICAN RED CROSS SURVEY ON SOCIAL MEDIA IN EMERGENCIES – JULY, 2010

The power of social media as a communications tool during disasters became clear to us in the aftermath of the earthquake in Haiti last year. The American Red Cross began receiving tweets from people trapped under collapsed buildings. Haiti lacked a responsive 9-1-1 system and with cell service down in the early hours, people sought help however they could.

Like many other disaster-relief organizations and emergency responders, the American Red Cross didn't have a good way to handle those pleas. We had to go through messages manually and try to route them to the right places. It was a sign to us that disaster response was being changed almost overnight by new technology.

So we decided to convene an Emergency Social Data Summit in August of last year to discuss this issue with other emergency response and disaster relief agencies, as well as the social media entities who were part of this growing phenomenon.

To inform the debate, the American Red Cross conducted a survey of web users, which showed many would turn to social communities to seek help for themselves or others during emergencies. And even more importantly, they expected first responders to be listening.

The online survey, conducted in July 2010, asked 1,058 adults about how they would use social media sites in emergency situations. The survey found that among web users, social media sites are the fourth most popular source for emergency information, just behind television news, radio and online news sites. More web users say they get their emergency information from social media than from a NOAA weather radio, government website or emergency text message system. One in five social media users also report posting eyewitness accounts of emergency events to their accounts.

The survey found that they would also use social media to ask for help. Our survey revealed that if people needed help and couldn't reach 9-1-1, one in five would try to contact responders through a digital means such as e-mail, websites or social media. If web users knew of someone else who needed help, 44 percent would ask other people in their social network to contact authorities, 35 percent would post a request for help directly on a response agency's Facebook page and 28 percent would send a Twitter message to responders.

The Red Cross survey last summer also suggested that Americans have high expectations about how first responders should be answering their requests. For example, 69 percent said that emergency responders should be monitoring social media sites in order to quickly send help—and nearly half believe a response agency is probably already responding to any urgent request they might see.

And the survey respondents expected quick responses to online appeals for assistance—74 percent expected help to come less than an hour after their tweet or Facebook post.

Those were some eye-opening expectations. And we know that they don't match reality.

Another survey, taken just a month before, of members of DomPrep40, an advisory board of disaster response practitioners and leaders, found that 9 in 10 of the respondent groups were not staffed to monitor or respond to requests via social media platforms during major events.

We know that the first and best choice for anyone in an emergency situation is to call 9-1-1. However, as was recently reported in the *Washington Post*,[1] 9-1-1 systems are slow to evolve in this digital age. When phone lines are down or the 9-1-1 system is overwhelmed, people will turn to social media.

---

[1] "Texting 911, Emergency Line Just Doesn't Get It." Sunday, April 24, 2011, the Washington Post.   http://www.washingtonpost.com/local/texting-911-emergency-line-just-doesnt-get-it/2011/03/28/AF3VKnXE story.html

EMERGENCY DATA SUMMIT – AUGUST 12, 2010

The Emergency Social Data Summit was convened by the Red Cross on August 12, 2010 in Washington, DC.

More than 150 people attended the all-day Summit to talk about how best we can all engage social media to improve upon disaster preparedness and our collective disaster response. And while 150 were in the building, another 1,200 contributed virtually to the conference via Ustream and Twitter. It was quite a sight to see people live-blogging and tweeting in the same Red Cross Headquarters where people once rolled bandages during World War I.

This gathering marked the first time that government, nonprofit, technology, and citizen sectors came together to discuss the opportunities and challenges we face in integrating social data with disaster response. This hearing today will give these issues even more prominence, and we appreciate your leadership in these discussions.

A wide range of ideas and questions came out of the day-long conference, with seven key questions emerging:

- What can we do to prepare in advance of a crisis?
- Who should have custody of emergency social data? How should it be used?
- Can we codify a solution for routing this data to the proper places?
- What about the issues of accessibility to social media among people with disabilities?
- How do we avoid duplication of effort in responding to pleas for help?
- What is the best way to authenticate requests?
- How do we manage citizen expectations for response?

After the summit, we prepared a document entitled, "The Path Forward." This overview examined some of the issues, opportunities and challenges surrounding each of these questions. I have attached a copy of that document to this testimony.

The questions identified after the Emergency Social Data Summit will not be answered today and will probably not be answered tomorrow. Nevertheless, as your Subcommittee engages in this important conversation about social media in disaster response, they present a good basis for the discussion.

Today, for the purposes of this hearing, I'd like to focus on how the American Red Cross is exploring social tools to assist us in meeting the needs of those affected by disaster.

THE AMERICAN RED CROSS AND SOCIAL MEDIA IN A DISASTER

For over 130 years, the American Red Cross has continued to operate in a constant cycle of responding to disasters and preparing for the next one. The tools we use to respond to disasters have evolved over the years – but perhaps the most exciting innovations are coming just now as we better understand the opportunities presented by advances in social technologies.

It may seem incongruous for an institution as old as ours to be embracing social media, but our experience teaches us that people in a crisis will communicate the same way they are used to communicating every day. Today, people are communicating with their family and friends on a daily basis through social media, so that is how the Red Cross must communicate. We currently have about 285,000 Facebook fans and 362,000 Twitter followers, and I am proud of the innovative work or team is doing to make social media a valuable part of our 21st century disaster response.

We use these tools to keep the public informed about relief efforts and to offer preparedness tips in real time. When a disaster occurs, we immediately acknowledge the situation by posting a status update to Facebook, a Tweet, a short video to YouTube, and a post to the Disaster Online Newsroom and our blog. We let our stakeholders know that we will update them with information about our relief efforts as they happen. While there's still much room for improvement, we have honed our standard operating procedures to provide nearly real-time information, action items, and tips.

We train Red Cross volunteers who deploy to disasters to use their smart phones and social technologies. These volunteers create new content from the field to better and more openly share the Red Cross relief efforts.

Mobile technologies and satellite communications are bringing everyone—humanitarian organizations, international institutions, volunteer technical communities, and the affected populations—ever closer together.

Using tools provided by social media partners such as Google Maps, the American Red Cross is collecting and compiling information that we never have been able to collect in the past. We are listening to those affected by disaster and we are sharing updates and information with partners and responders. We are building social media into our operational DNA.

GETTING HELP

The Red Cross uses these tools to empower our stakeholders to get help or give help.

First, getting help. As indicated in our survey, increasing numbers of people rely on their social community during crises. More often than not, victims of disasters can communicate via text messages, Twitter and Facebook in real time.

We have built a dynamic shelter map using Google maps to update our open shelter information every 30 minutes. We provide this information to the public through a public-facing portal and map on *www.redcross.org*. We also built an iPhone app so people on the move can access shelter information.

We are in the process of creating an official digital volunteer role that will help monitor, authenticate and route incoming disaster requests and information to other colleagues and partners. This kind of training allows remote employees and colleagues to assist in the disaster response efforts too. Colleagues using hash tags like #crisisdata, #redcross or something similar can collect, collate and respond to queries and concerns from their own homes.

GIVING HELP

Second, we use social media tools to empower people to give help. Our mobile fundraising efforts have made it easier than ever for donors to make donations with a text. We first saw the power of texting after the earthquake in Haiti when we raised more than $32 million dollars via text - $10 at a time. Forty-one percent of donors were under age 34 indicating a new generation was giving, perhaps for the first time in their lives.

We have partnered with Facebook Causes to allow for donations within Facebook, and we've worked with Twitter to make it easy for people to give there, too. We are transparent as possible, give our stakeholders digital tools, and they are easily able to help inspire their own networks to become part of our mission.

PREVENTING AND PREPARING FOR AN EMERGENCY

In Haiti, the Red Cross saw 4 million SMS text messages successfully delivered to approximately half a million Haitians as part of the cholera response. Messages covered the symptoms of cholera, treatment and simple steps to prevent it, people learned about preparedness measures, how to clean drainage around their homes to reduce the risk of flooding; and store reserves of water, food and medicine. The campaign also promoted the free Haitian Red Cross recorded information line, which received 400,000 calls.

Domestically, text messages and alert systems allow for citizens to receive aggregate information and news alerts from emergency response agencies and other media outlets. The public can be instantly informed about emergency situations, weather hazards and what actions should be taken to respond to that emergency. These alerts are pushed out further through social media. And citizen reports supplement this information and provide responders with additional situational awareness.

This expansion of warning systems is exemplified in many communities like in King County, Seattle where the Regional Public Information Network keeps the public informed about potential hazards and offers updates on emergency response. The network is also integrated with 9-1-1 and the local fire dispatch log.

Mr. Chairman, as you and your colleagues continue to explore the possibilities of social media, the answers to some of your questions will be found at the local level. We believe a local response is the most effective response because it all begins with individuals, families and communities.

GAINING SITUATIONAL AWARENESS

When geodata is included in messages or when pictures are attached to a message – responders learn more about size, scope and necessary response for that location. This can prove to be a valuable tool in damage assessment following a disaster.

This operational data is important in how we approach reporting of sheltering activities. American Red Cross relief operations identify all locations and populations for all shelters and ensure this data is entered into the National Shelter System (NSS) database. The Red Cross NSS information is available through a downloadable application and contains location and capacity information for over 56,000 community facilities (schools, churches, etc.) that have been established as potential shelters across the country. The system records all shelter openings, closings and overnight populations on a daily basis, and is used to guide operational and planning decisions for multiple agencies at all levels. These comprehensive reporting practices and improved access to information allow us to more effectively identify and assess the needs of those affected by disasters as well as provide invaluable resources and information to the public seeking help.

KEEPING FAMILIES CONNECTED

In the first hours after a disaster strikes, an initial concern is to inform and connect family and friends. The American Red Cross is able to facilitate family communication through its Safe and Well website, found on www.RedCross.org. Here, individuals in affected areas may register their well-being using messages that can be seen by family and friends located outside the disaster area inquiring about their loved one's safety. Disaster victims also may update their Facebook and Twitter status through the Safe and Well website. Additionally, smart phone users may visit *www.redcross.org/safeandwell* and click on the "List Yourself as Safe and Well" or "Search for friends and family" link.

CORRECTING MISINFORMATION

During the Summit, those gathered considered the need to authenticate and verify information. There is a balance between acting on information shared through social media outlets and ensuring what is transpired is accurate and correct. Because Red Cross colleagues are watching, tracking and engaging in social media during times of disaster, we are also quick to respond when misinformation is posted. We can often squelch misinformation quickly and decisively as we authenticate and verify information.

BUILDING RESILIENCE

FEMA Administrator Craig Fugate often speaks of his goal to have people see themselves as survivors and not victims of a disaster. "Social media can empower the public to be a part of the response, not victims to be taken care of." Social media enables neighbors to be a first responder to the immediate needs of their neighbors.

In catastrophic disasters we almost always see an abundance of hope from the unaffected – people want to tangibly help. We haven't previously been able to provide limitless valuable roles for these people, but with technology advances there are many opportunities to do just this, turning that abundance of care into more resilient communities, more effective disaster response, and more valuable partnerships.

CONCLUSION

Mr. Chairman and Members of the Subcommittee, thank you again for this opportunity to provide testimony today. We are excited to be working with this Subcommittee and your Congressional colleagues to explore the opportunities presented by engaging social media in our disaster preparedness and response.

The American Red Cross is committed to using all the tools of social media to improve our disaster response, but I would like to end with several thoughts:

If there is one thing that we've learned on this recent journey it is that we must continue to embrace change and remain open to new ideas and new platforms. Next year we may not be talking about Facebook or Twitter – but something entirely different. We need to be flexible and nimble.

And, if there's one thing that still must be addressed – it is a discussion of a potential increased role of Federal government. How can government better facilitate use of social media and new technologies to improve upon preparedness and disaster response?

The 2010 Summit participants were passionate about the need for a central, uniform system juxtaposed with *multiple* potential responsible parties including local responders, state agencies, nonprofits and, of course, the Federal government. Much discussion centered around the notion of porting data directly into the 911 system. The technical issues with texting are numerous and would require greater standardization by the entire wireless industry. While such a change could take years, some participants believe that intermediate steps could be taken to more easily share data between various agencies, local government and aid groups.

Finally, technology is a tool, not an end in itself. Our goal is to help alleviate human suffering and ensure that the country is as prepared as possible to respond to any disaster. We will use technology to do that, but it is not about the technology, it is about the people we serve.

Thank you again for your leadership. I am happy to address any questions you may have.

In: Social Media and Disasters   ISBN: 978-1- 61942-461-6
Editors: T. F. Sykes and E. A. Travis   © 2012 Nova Science Publishers, Inc

Chapter 5

TESTIMONY OF SHONA L. BROWN, SENIOR VICE PRESIDENT, GOOGLE.ORG, BEFORE THE SENATE COMMITTEE ON HOMELAND SECURITY AND GOVERNMENTAL AFFAIRS. HEARING ON "UNDERSTANDING THE POWER OF SOCIAL MEDIA AS A COMMUNICATION TOOL IN THE AFTERMATH OF DISASTERS" [*]

Chairman Pryor, Ranking Member Brown,
and Members of the Committee.

Thank you for your focus on the important issue of crisis response and the central role that technology now plays in disaster relief and recovery. During the past year, tens of millions of people around the world have suffered through natural disasters such as earthquakes in Haiti, Japan, Chile, China, and New Zealand; floods in Pakistan and Australia; and forest fires in Israel. Our own citizens have faced crises, with tornadoes and floods causing terrible

---

[*] This is an edited, reformatted and augmented version of testimony given by Shona L. Brown, Senior Vice President, Google.org, before the Senate Homeland Security Ad Hoc Subcommittee on Disaster Recovery and Intergovernmental Affairs, Hearing on "Understanding the Power of Social Media as a Communication Tool in the Aftermath of Disasters", on May 5, 2011.

damage in recent weeks reminding us of the toll natural disasters have on human life. Our thoughts are with the communities that have just been hit by devastating tornadoes in Alabama and across the US.

As the Senior Vice President of Google.org, the philanthropic arm of Google, which includes the team that responds to natural disasters around the world, I have seen the increasing importance of Internet -based technologies in crisis response. Our team has used search and geographic-based tools to respond to over 20 crises in over 10 languages since Hurricane Katrina, and we have already responded to more crises in 2011 than we did all of last year. In the aftermath of the devastating tornadoes in Alabama last week, we supported the Red Cross by providing maps that locate nearby shelters, updated satellite imagery for first responders, and directed local users searching for "tornado" or "twister" to the maps through an enhanced search result.

Our work is modest in comparison to the work of emergency relief organizations and governments that are called to action, and our team does not claim to be expert in crisis response. We are computer scientists and developers, and Google.org is a newcomer to this space. We are still learning how we can help to respond to different types of crises. But our experiences have given us a unique vantage point on how powerful and robust a resource Internet-based technologies can be for both emergency responders and affected populations as they prepare for, respond to, and recover from a disaster. Here's why:

First, the Internet often remains available when other networks fail. The Internet was designed to be robust in the face of outages, and to automatically reroute through the path of least resistance. Its openness and interoperability continue to enable communication and access to information even when disasters render other means of communication unavailable. As a result, Internet-based emergency tools have proved to be quite reliable in disasters.

Time and time again, the Internet has served as a medium of communication when voice and text services are overburdened. Even when there is no power to boot up a computer, people are able to access the Internet through mobile devices to find emergency information or share their whereabouts.

Second, simple Internet technologies are often more effective than purpose-built technologies in emergencies. Google's products were not built as emergency-response tools, but we've found that they can be helpful in disasters. In emergency after emergency we see use of Google Search spike dramatically in affected areas, led by searches for information ranging from the status of loved ones to trustworthy information. Gmail and other Internet-based services like Google Maps are the tools of choice for many emergency responders who must be able to access email and documents anywhere in the world using whatever kind of operating system or connectivity they find. And Google Maps allows many response organizations to determine where to allocate resources. Organization smay, for example, use a familiar tool like Google Maps to make sure they set up their clinic next to a refugee center. This is because these technologies are simple, use common standards,and allow for open access.

Third, the Internet scales and allows different devices and applications to work together. The Internet Protocol has scalability at its core. This means that when demand increases to exceptional levels in an emergency, the Internet can handle it. Other communications networks are engineered with normal use patterns in mind and become overwhelmed quickly when these expectations are upset by disaster. The Internet Protocol also has openness in its DNA. An array of devices, using untold numbers of different applications, can all work together because of the way the Internet was built. These two strengths mean that the Internet allows tools created in response to one emergency to be rapidly iterated to fit the needs of a different emergency. For example, it took Google only 72 hours to create the Google Person Finder after the earthquake in Haiti. We managed to push the tool live just 90 minutes after the earthquake hit in Japan and made over 22 improvements to the tool during the crisis. This level of rapid iteration is something that is unique to Internet applications.

With these advantages of Internet-based technologies in mind, I would like to discuss the impact of three Google projects in recent relief efforts around the world: (1) Google Earth/Maps, (2) Person Finder, and (3) our efforts to make relevant news and information more readily available, such as through Crisis Response Landing Pages and enhanced search results.

GOOGLE EARTH/MAPS

In the emergency context, Google Earth, Google Maps, and Google MapMaker help organizations visualize assets geographically and make it easier for the affected population to find nearby emergency resources. Updated satellite imagery allows for quick damage assessments from thousands of miles away and can help relief organizations navigate disaster zones with, for example, crowdsourced information on available roads.

Last year's 7.0 magnitude earthquake in Haiti prompted us to scale existing tools to assist relief organizations. Organizations often use Google Earth and Maps to develop targeted relief plans, so we updated high resolution satellite imagery from our partner GeoEye within 24 hours of the earthquake and were the first to make such imagery available for public use. In addition, we collected 15-cm-resolution aerial imagery—much cleaner than a satellite can capture—of the affected region. This imagery has been used to conduct wide-scale damage assess ments, plan response and recovery efforts such as clinic and hospital placements, and raise worldwide awareness of disasters.

A small Google team traveled to Haiti to better understand how our tools can be useful. We embedded with the 82nd Airborne in a refugee camp in what used to be the Petionville Golf Course. Soldiers from the 82nd used Google Maps to plan the routes they would take while patrolling the area. One of the officers explained to our team that they used Google Maps because "they use tools they're used to."

We found the same to be true after the terrible recent flooding in Pakistan. In the US, we tend to take complete maps for granted. Long before the flooding, two Pakistani web developers decided that available maps of their country were inadequate. So they decided to fix that situation with Google MapMaker, and along the way became some of the top volunteer mappers in the world. All their work played a major role in

helping Pakistanis in the aftermath of the floods last August, when 20 percent of Pakistan was underwater. In response to the emergency, we shared our MapMaker base data with UNOSAT, which is the United Nations' mapping agency. This mapping information was helpful to emergency responders working in that terrible disaster.

These two examples show how Google's flexible, familiar, Internet-based mapping technologies can be quite powerful in a crisis. And more recently, in the wake of the tornadoes in the Southeast US, we requested satellite updates from partners and published a map layer with any useful data we could find about the tornadoes.

Many other organizations have taken advantage of the open Internet and the ability to crowdsource information in order to do incredible mapping work. Open Street Map, for example, has been credited with making the most complete map of Haiti's roads ever by getting the Haitian Diaspora to volunteer their knowledge. Ushahidi, another technology nonprofit, also allows for the creation of maps illustrating, for example, political violence in Kenya that people report through Twitter, email, or SMS.

PERSON FINDER

Now I'll turn to Person Finder. Person Finder is an open-source web-based application that allows individuals to check and post on the status of relatives or friends affected by a disaster. Before Person Finder was developed, those seeking missing loved ones had to sift through multiple websites, posting the same inquiries over and over, hoping that the person they were seeking happened to register with one of these websites. In Haiti, for example, we noticed that there were 14 different missing persons databases. They were not integrated, all were running on different infrastructure, and all had a different amount of data that together represented all missing persons records.

To make this process more effective and efficient, while continuing to leverage the power of crowdsourced information, our team built Google Person Finder to act as a central database, pushing and pulling the feeds from all 14 databases, and allowing users to search across the information in all of the databases. Google Person Finder accepts information in a common machine-readable format called PFIF (People Finder Interchange Format), which was created by Hurricane Katrina volunteers in 2005. Our team worked around the clock to build and launch Person Finder in less than 72 hours during the early days of the crisis in Haiti. We have now made this resource available in more than 42 languages.

While we've used Person Finder for several disasters over the past year, the 9.0 magnitude earthquake and tsunami that struck the Tohoku region of Japan on March 11 led to its biggest use. People around the world struggled to connect with their loved ones as telecommunications services flickered. With phone and SMS networks overburdened by traffic, it was difficult to find out if loved ones were alive and well. But the Internet generally continued to function well, and Person Finder became a critical tool.

The product is purposefully simple, fast, and easy to use. More importantly, it is backed by an open programmatic interface, or API. This means that different sites can update missing persons lists automatically using the common format. Because of this, The New York Times, CNN, NPR, and a number of other websites quickly integrated Person Finder, increasing the reach and resulting in a more complete list of missing persons.

Today, Person Finder is a completely open source tool with a healthy discussion group and numerous external contributors. Person Finder helped manage more than 55,000 records of missing persons in Haiti, 75,000 records in Chile, and more than 600,000 records after the earthquake in Japan. We saw over 36 million pageviews in the first 48 hours after that earthquake. That number is likely overwhelming to most organizations and even government agencies, but we have the infrastructure to handle that volume.

Our own Senior Product Manager Kei Kawai lives in California and was trying to get in touch with his family back in Japan after the earthquake. He confirmed each person's safety, but could not make contact with his wife's grandfather, who lives in a town called Soma City that largely got washed out by the tsunami. After posting to Google Person Finder, Kei was relieved when news arrived through a post on Person Finder the next day that his wife's grandfather was safe.

CENTRALIZED INFORMATION POINTS

The third Google project I'd like to discuss relates to getting affected populations up-to-the-minute information as a crisis unfolds. As I mentioned earlier, we know from past experience that people turn to the Web for information during crises. Within a few hours of the Japan earthquake, we placed an alert on the Google homepage for Tsunami alerts in the Pacific and ran similar promotions across News, Maps, and other services. As a Tsunami warning was also issued for Hawaii, we saw a massive spike in search queries originating from Hawaii related to "tsunami."

With so many people searching online for critical information, we added an enhanced search result so that people could connect with emergency information as easily as possible. For example, someone in Japan who did a Google search for their town name plus the word "blackout" would have seen the scheduled blackout information above the typical search results. This information was not easily available before our work and we had to scrape numerous government websites and convert the data into machine readable formats. In the case of the recent tornadoes in the US, we enabled enhanced search results for Alabama and surrounding states with a link to the maps. The enhanced results appe ar when local users search for "tornado" or "twister."

Access to and use of Google search is generally widespread and many people turn to us in emergencies. As a result, we often create central crisis response sites where information such as emergency numbers, access to temporary shelters, news updates, maps, videos, user generated content, and donation opportunities are aggregated. Millions of people visit these landing pages which are created in a matter of hours and sometimes linked to on the country specific Google homepage. Those seeking information on an emergency generally fall into three categories. First, people directly affected who are looking for information such as power outages, temporary shelter, and how to respond. Second, people indirectly affected looking for family in the area or looking to share useful information. And third, aid organizations looking for imagery, to coordinate their response, and for logistical assistance. Our landing pages seek to assist each group. Furthermore, these pages allow people around the world to learn more and make donations. Our past landing pages have driven many millions of dollars of donations to relief organizations.

HOW GOVERNMENTS CAN SUPPORT TECHNOLOGY EFFORTS IN CRISIS RESPONSE

Now that I've discussed how Google is approaching the use of technology in emergencies, I'd like to discuss one big way that governments and other organizations can support these and future efforts—by maintaining and even enhancing the openness and interoperability of the information available on the Internet.

An open and interoperable Internet allowed users to track the recent Australian floods on an interactive map because the map used the Keyhole Markup Language (KML), a machine readable and crawlable format used to describe geographic information. An open standard, namely the People Finder Interchange Format, or PFIF, also allows Person Finder to access and coordinate more than a dozen different databases, which gave those seeking family and friends in Japan access to more than 600,000 records.

But openness and interoperability do not characterize all parts of the Internet. The ability of the Internet to capitalize on its potential of assisting in crises depends on both companies and governments improving how they share information. Using divergent standards slows collaboration and response time. But speedy and open access, powering the ability of users to share and communicate information, accelerates relief efforts.

To pursue some of the projects I've described, Google had to gather emergency information from government websites in arcane formats and then translate them into open standards. Sometimes the information was spread across numerous websites. Other times, the licensing status of the data was not readily apparent. And even today, some important data is not even online at all, but is in someone's spreadsheet on their personal computer.

On the other hand, for example, the open KML standard, allows people to quickly create maps about shelter locations, escape routes, and emergency plans—and it is so easy to use that you don't have to be an expert developer to build a map. Governments and NGOs such as the Red Cross that maintain such lists could use KML, and if they inform us when they surface this information in advance of a disaster, we could feature it on our pages. It helps if this collaboration occurs in advance of a disaster, not in the middle of an emergency.

Similarly the PFIF allows organizations and users to easily upload information with a common format and to speak a simple common language so we can identify individuals in a consistent manner, making it simple for computers to automate the process of syncing multiple databases. Without this open platform and common standard, efforts to find missing persons become less coordinated and far more taxing on all parties. We ask organizations with missing persons databases to adopt the PFIF standard and encourage local governments and police to use PFIF as well. The troubling truth is that many organizations gathering missing persons information—as well as other critical data such as public health information—continue to do so on paper. The result is that we find boxes of unprocessed forms sitting in offices long after we have lost the chance to use them to help people. Wide adoption of PFIF can help.

And lastly, we recommend adoption of better alerting systems that leverage the Common Alerting Protocol (CAP) standard to quickly inform users of impending crises such as tsunamis and everyday alerts including transit delays. The Integrated Public Alert and Warning System operated by the Department of Homeland Security is a great first step. Agencies such as NOAA, for weather alerting, and USGS, for earthquake notifications, have done a great job being early adopters of CAP, but they require resources to improve the initial work they've done and allow for a truly robust Internet based warning system.

With better alerting systems, if they are implemented in an open and interoperable fashion, private actors such as Google could interact with government systems to display alerts tailored to geography, vulnerability, and situation. And we could do so in an open manner so any other Internet company or emergency organization could use or build on it.

CONCLUSION

I would like to conclude by thanking Chairman Pryor, Ranking Member Brown, the members of the Senate Committee on Homeland Security and other Members of Congress who have taken an interest in technology and crisis response. We will continue to work to help users instantly find the information they need when crises hit. We recommend the adoption of simple, open, and standard ways of publishing and disseminating information. And we look forward to working with you, government agencies, and emergency relief organizations. We play a modest role in comparison to the actors who work on emergency relief as their core mission, but we will cont inue to try and improve the use of Internet-based technologies for preparedness, response, and recovery, whether the emergency is a Pacific tsunami or tornadoes in the South.

In: Social Media and Disasters ISBN: 978-1- 61942-461-6
Editors: T. F. Sykes and E. A. Travis © 2012 Nova Science Publishers, Inc

Chapter 6

TESTIMONY OF HEATHER BLANCHARD, CO-FOUNDER OF CRISISCOMMONS, BEFORE THE SENATE COMMITTEE ON HOMELAND SECURITY AND GOVERNMENTAL AFFAIRS. HEARING ON "UNDERSTANDING THE POWER OF SOCIAL MEDIA AS A COMMUNICATION TOOL IN THE AFTERMATH OF DISASTERS"[*]

Good morning Chairman Pryor, Ranking Member Brown, and distinguished members of the Subcommittee. My name is Heather Blanchard, and I am a co-founder of CrisisCommons, a volunteer technology community that connects people and organizations who use open data and technology to innovate crisis management and global development. Before this position, I spent seven years at the U.S. Department of Homeland Security, including Deputy Director of the Ready Campaign. On behalf of our community, it is a true honor to testify before you today.

When a crisis occurs, it isn't emergency responders who are first on the scene. It's everyday people who use everyday resources like their mobile

---

[*] This is an edited, reformatted and augmented version of testimony given by Heather Blanchard, Co Founder of CrisisCommons before the Ad Hoc Subcommittee on Disaster Recovery and Intergovernmental Affairs, Homeland Security and Governmental Affairs Committee, United States Senate, on May 5, 2011.

phone and social networks to share what they know. This could be a road blocked by a tree after a storm or creating a map of where they see wildfires. Today, there are many volunteers who leverage technology, like CrisisCommons, that can direct technical capacity, harness open data and collaborative tools to help first responders and communities make sense from the deluge of information that occurs in a crisis. We believe that information at the right time and right place can help response authorities and citizens make better decisions especially in a crisis.

Since the spring of 2009, CrisisCommons has been an open forum to explore how information, including social media, can help in a crisis. Our community has supported organizations and citizens in the response to the Haiti and Japan earthquakes, Tennessee floods, and last week's historic tornados which impacted the south east. Just to share an example, during the blizzard which paralyzed Chicago this year, our volunteers through CrisisCampChicago in collaboration with Humanity Road supported the Chicago Tribune Snow Map to assure that public requests for assistance were routed to 311 and other local authorities. One challenge we often see is that government agencies simplify the use of social media as a public affairs function when in fact, during a crisis, access to citizen-generated information is an operational necessity. As an example, this year during our support for the National Level Exercise the situational awareness workgroup that we participated in struggled to define how social media information would be coordinated from an operational perspective as there is not a resourced function which connects open data, including social media, and leverages potential surge capacity from communities like CrisisCommons. We would like to recommend to the committee that government create an operational liaison function which connects volunteer technology communities to our response systems at the Federal, State and local levels and be resourced for support during steady state and in crisis events. We recommend that current emergency management doctrine be revised to include the capability to harness technology volunteer expertise and collaborative systems.

Another challenge we have observed, is that in local Emergency Operations Centers the connection between social media information and operations is largely absent. We were shocked to find that some centers lacked high bandwidth Internet, technical skills or collaborative tools. We were also dismayed to find that many agencies have stringent security policies blocking their workforce from using social media tools for operational purposes. Without this capability emergency managers could be missing critical information in their operational picture. We recommend that emergency management infrastructure be fully modernized. We also recommend that policy and incident management doctrine be modified to allow emergency management personnel to engage outside of their own organizational networks to take advantage of social media tools and capabilities.

As you can see, emergency management is not prepared to utilize social media tools and data to augment their operations and inform their mission priorities. When there is a crisis, emergency management continuously find themselves overwhelmed with information. We recommend that resources be devoted towards helping emergency managers with data preparedness and filtering, increasing the level of digital literacy of the emergency management workforce and empowering their ability to connect with technology support.

In looking at the government's role in this ecosystem, the days of agencies passively sitting on the social media sidelines from behind the firewall are over. The time has come to evolve to a more open and participatory crisis management model. We believe that the Federal government has a leadership role to play but again, we feel that institutional support is needed to move us to the next level. To emphasize we recommend the following:

- Create an operational liaison function to coordinate with volunteer technology communities
- Revise policy and incident management doctrine to incorporate social media and other technology capabilities
- Invest in modernization of emergency management infrastructure and collaborative tools
- Support data preparedness and filtering, increasing the level of digital literacy of the emergency management workforce and empowering their ability to connect with technology support.

In spite of these challenges, we know of many emergency managers who are pushing the envelope everyday, sometimes at a professional risk, to apply social media tools and data in their work. We are supportive of enlightened leadership that Administrator Fugate displays everyday. He has opened the door to discussion and experimentation that we see today. However, individuals cannot change institutional challenges by example. Today we are asking for your help to support the needed enhancements that emergency management needs to fully utilize social media information and providing connectivity to communities who can support their efforts like CrisisCommons.

Thank you very much for the opportunity to testify before you today. I look forward to answering any questions you may have.

In: Social Media and Disasters   ISBN: 978-1- 61942-461-6
Editors: T. F. Sykes and E. A. Travis   © 2012 Nova Science Publishers, Inc

Chapter 7

PERSONAL LOCALIZED ALERTING NETWORK (PLAN) FACT SHEET[*]

BACKGROUND

Have you ever thought that, for emergency alerts to be distributed as quickly as possible, they should be sent to cell phones? The Federal Communications Commission (FCC), along with the Federal Emergency Management Agency (FEMA) and the wireless industry, is working to make that possible.

WHAT IS THE PERSONAL LOCALIZED ALERTING NETWORK (PLAN)?

PLAN is a new public safety system that allows customers who own an enabled mobile device to receive geographically-targeted, text-like messages alerting them of imminent threats to safety in their area. The new technology ensures that emergency alerts will not get stuck in highly congested user areas, which can happen with standard mobile voice and texting services.

PLAN enables government officials to target emergency alerts to specific geographic areas through cell towers (*e.g.* lower Manhattan), which pushes the information to dedicated receivers in PLAN-enabled mobile devices.

---

[*] Citation note: The Fact Sheet below was taken from the following Federal Communications Commission (FCC) website on 9/27/11:   http://www.fcc.gov/guides/personal-localized-alerting-network-plan

PLAN complements the existing Emergency Alert System (EAS) which is implemented by the FCC and FEMA at the federal level through broadcasters and other media service providers. Like the EAS, PLAN is intended to keep up with new technologies that can keep Americans safer.

Wireless companies volunteer to participate in PLAN – technically called the Commercial Mobile Alert System (CMAS). PLAN is the result of a unique public/private partnership between the FCC, FEMA and the wireless industry with the singular objective of enhanced public safety.

Participating wireless carriers must begin deployment of PLAN by April 7, 2012. Some carriers – AT&T, Sprint, T-Mobile and Verizon -- will offer PLAN in certain areas ahead of schedule.

HOW DOES PLAN WORK?

Authorized national, state or local government officials send alerts regarding public safety emergencies, such as a tornado or a terrorist threat to PLAN.

PLAN authenticates the alert, verifies that the sender is authorized and sends it to participating wireless carriers.

Participating wireless carriers push the alerts from cell towers to mobile devices in the affected area. The alerts appear like text messages on mobile devices. Participating wireless service providers must be able to target alerts to individual counties, and ensure that alerts reach customers roaming outside a provider's service area.

WHO WILL RECEIVE
PLAN ALERTS?

Alerts are geographically targeted, so a customer living in downtown New York would not receive a threat if they happen to be in Chicago when the alert is sent. Similarly, someone visiting downtown New York from Chicago on that same day would receive the alert. This requires a PLAN enabled mobile device and participation by the wireless provider in PLAN.

HOW MUCH WILL CONSUMERS PAY TO RECEIVE PLAN ALERTS?

Alerts are free. Customers do not pay to receive PLAN alerts.

DO CONSUMERS HAVE TO SIGN UP TO RECEIVE ALERTS?

Customers of participating carriers are automatically signed up. PLAN allows government officials to send emergency alerts to all subscribers with PLAN-capable devices if their wireless carrier participates in the program. Consumers do not need to sign up for this service.

WHAT ALERTS WILL PLAN DELIVER?

Alerts from PLAN cover only critical emergency alerts. Consumers will receive only three types of alerts:

1) Alerts issued by the President
2) Alerts involving imminent threats to safety or life
3) Amber Alerts

Participating carriers may allow subscribers to block all but Presidential alerts.

WHAT WILL CONSUMERS EXPERIENCE WHEN THEY RECEIVE A PLAN ALERT?

PLAN uses a unique signal and vibration, and appears much like a text message. A PLAN alert will be accompanied by a unique attention signal and vibration, which is particularly helpful to people with hearing or vision-related disabilities. The PLAN alert will appear as a pop-up text on the handset screen much like a text message.

WILL CONSUMERS BE ABLE TO RECEIVE
PLAN ALERTS ON A PREPAID PHONE?

Yes. Consumers with prepaid phones can receive PLAN alerts as long as their provider has decided to participate in PLAN and the customer has a PLAN-enabled device. Such consumers will receive PLAN alerts just as customers with postpaid, monthly service will.

WILL PLAN TRACK MY LOCATION?

No. PLAN is not designed to – and does not – track the location of anyone receiving a PLAN alert.

ARE PLAN ALERTS TEXT MESSAGES?

No. PLAN messages are not text messages. Alerts will not have to be opened like SMS text messages, but will "pop up" on the device's screen. PLAN alerts are transmitted using a new technology that is separate and different from voice calls and SMS text messages. This new technology ensures that emergency alerts will not get stuck in highly congested user areas, which can happen with standard mobile voice and texting services.

WILL CONSUMERS NEED A NEW PHONE
OR A SMART PHONE TO RECEIVE ALERTS?

Some phones may require only software upgrades to receive alerts, while in other cases a subscriber may need to purchase a new PLAN-capable device. Consumers should check with their wireless carrier regarding the availability of PLAN-capable handsets.

WILL PLAN BE AVAILABLE EVERYWHERE?

Participation in PLAN by wireless carriers is voluntary. Some carriers will offer PLAN over all or parts of their service areas or over all or only some of their wireless devices. Ultimately, we expect that PLAN will be available in most of the country. Consumers should check with their wireless carriers to determine the extent to which they are offering PLAN.

CAN CONSUMERS BLOCK PLAN ALERTS?

Partially. Participating wireless carriers may offer subscribers with PLAN-capable handsets the ability to block alerts involving imminent threats to safety of life and/or AMBER Alerts; however, consumers cannot block emergency alerts issued by the President.

HOW WILL SUBSCRIBERS KNOW IF THEIR CARRIER OFFERS PLAN?

The FCC requires all wireless carriers that do not participate in PLAN to notify customers. Consumers should check with their wireless carriers to determine the extent to which they are offering PLAN.

In: Social Media and Disasters
Editors: T. F. Sykes and E. A. Travis

ISBN: 978-1- 61942-461-6
© 2012 Nova Science Publishers, Inc

Chapter 8

PRIVACY IMPACT ASSESSMENT FOR THE USE OF UNIDIRECTIONAL SOCIAL MEDIA APPLICATIONS COMMUNICATIONS AND OUTREACH[*]

ABSTRACT

Unidirectional social media applications encompass a range of applications, often referred to as applets or widgets,[1] that allow users to view relevant, real-time content from predetermined sources.[2] The Department of Homeland Security (DHS or Department) intends to use unidirectional social media tools including desktop widgets, mobile apps,[3] podcasts,[4] audio and video streams,[5] Short Message Service (SMS) texting,[6] and Really Simple Syndication[7] (RSS) feeds, among others, for external relations (communications and outreach) and to disseminate timely content to the public about DHS initiatives, public safety, and other official activities and one-way notifications. These dynamic communication tools broaden the Department's ability to disseminate content and provide the public multiple channels to receive and view content. The public will continue to have the option of obtaining comparable content and services through the Department's official websites and other official means. This Privacy Impact Assessment (PIA) analyzes the Department's use of unidirectional social media applications. This PIA does not cover users sending content to the Department. Additionally, this PIA will describe the personally

---

[*] This is an edited, reformatted and augmented version of a Department of Homeland Security publication, dated March 8, 2011.

identifiable information (PII) and the extremely limited circumstances that the Department will have access to PII, how it will use the PII, what PII is retained and shared, and how individuals can gain access to their PII. Appendix A of this PIA will serve as a listing, to be updated periodically, of DHS unidirectional social media applications, approved by the Chief Privacy Officer, that follow the requirements and analytical understanding outlined in this PIA.[8] The unidirectional social media applications listed in Appendix A are subject to Privacy Compliance Reviews by the DHS Privacy Office.

OVERVIEW

In accordance with the President's Memorandum on Transparency and Open Government (January 21, 2009)[9] and the Director of the Office of Management and Budget's (OMB) Open Government Directive Memorandum (December 8, 2009),[10] unidirectional social media applications provide DHS alternative opportunities to disseminate content to the public. These dynamic communications tools provide the public channels to access real-time content and download current content. The Department uses these government and non-government owned applications for external relations (communications and outreach) and to disseminate timely content to the public about DHS initiatives, public safety, and other official activities and notifications. DHS may use these unidirectional applications to inform the public on a range of topics such as: 1) airport security processing; 2) access to and security at federal buildings; 3) man-made and natural disaster preparedness; 4) transportation security; 5) pandemic planning/response; 6) border access and security; and 7) other public safety purposes as appropriate.

DHS uses unidirectional social media applications developed by components and third parties to make relevant content easily available in real-time to members of the public. Widgets function by streaming DHS authorized content to a Graphical User Interface (GUI) 11 and may have a frequent "refresh rate." Some have static content. Podcasts, another type of unidirectional social media application used by DHS, stream pre-recorded audio files to desktops, PDAs, and other internet-enabled devices. The same is true for RSS feeds and SMS text messages; they are unidirectional conveyors of content. In all cases the user must request that the application or service be initiated on their behalf so that they may receive desired communications from the Department. The Department will only "push" content to individuals by unidirectional social media applications who have subscribed to the particular product used by the Department to distribute official content.

Widgets permit users of website content to separate the content from the website and consume it in other places. For example, users can grab the widget code and drop it in another website and then have content in that widget update dynamically by DHS and automatically republish to any website where it appears. An RSS feed similarly allows the user to subscribe to published content on a website and have it appear in the client-side RSS reader, so the user can get real-time alerts whenever new content is posted to the website where the RSS feed resides. Podcasts and video-streams are audio and video feeds that typically are hosted on another server, either at DHS or with a third-party provider, may contain an embedded feature where the user can insert the code to appear in multiple websites from the same source. The distributed environment of these tools is largely responsible for the experience of allowing content to spread quickly across the Internet or "go viral." At the same time it allows the content creator to have good controls over the original content so that it is updated once and appears many times in many places.

Unidirectional social media applications may be developed by the Department or owned by third parties not affiliated with DHS. However, the government may place content on these third party websites or applications as long as the same content is available on a Department website. These unidirectional social media applications continue to grow in numbers and capability. Because of the depth and diversity of this reach, the Department is planning for the use of a multitude of unidirectional social media applications.

In many cases, the owners of the widgets used or developed by DHS to distribute official content do not require the user to create an account as a condition for accessing content. In the event that the widget owner requires a user account the user may be required to provide PII which will be transmitted to the widget owner and may be displayed to the user during any subsequent interactions with the widget. Some unidirectional social media applications run on an individual user's GUI and require specific information about the device and PII about the user in order to function correctly. For example, an application might require a user to input certain preferences including technical information and PII in order to customize the display of the application. A widget used to alert users about local emergencies, for instance, will ask for the individual to provide a zip code in order to provide geographic information relevant to the a specific location. The individual is not required to provide his actual zip code, only the information to enable DHS to provide the user with geographically specific content. DHS will not have access to the user preferences or technical device information. The Department will access and use unidirectional social media applications using only DHS-owned network assets.

It is imperative that the Department be transparent about its use of unidirectional social media applications to avoid concerns about government intrusion. The Department will engage in the use of uni-directional social media applications in a manner that protects privacy and respects the intent of users. In order to address these and other concerns, DHS has set forth specific requirements in this PIA regarding how the Department may use unidirectional social media applications in a privacy sensitive way. In advance of using unidirectional social media applications for purposes of distributing DHS content where the following applies, DHS shall:

1) Examine the privacy policy of the application owner and the application itself, if one is available, to evaluate the risks and to determine whether the application is appropriate for the Department's use;

2) Make available a privacy notice on the unidirectional social media application itself prior to using it as a distribution channel for DHS content;[12] and

3) Unless otherwise directed by statute, executive order, or regulation the Department's public affairs officials will serve as the primary account holders for all unidirectional social media applications hosted on third party sites across the Department and will manage and approve all DHS content disseminated through these public-facing applications. All content sent through official Department applications must be approved by the Department's public affairs officials prior to its dissemination. 13 The Department's public affairs officials will ensure that all disseminated content falls within the appropriate requirements for publicly available content and materials. OPA will, when necessary, act as the final authority on what content is acceptable for posting. Additionally, official DHS unidirectional social media applications will be identified by the Department's seal, when technologically possible.

When using approved unidirectional social media applications for purposes of distributing DHS content where the following applies, DHS shall:

1) Not require subscribers to provide PII to DHS as a condition of receiving content via unidirectional social media applications;
2) Establish user names easily identifiable as DHS accounts; and
3) Label/tag unidirectional social media applications with an official DHS logo.

This PIA outlines the Department's use of unidirectional social media applications and their intended use for external relations (communications and outreach) and as a means to disseminate timely content to the public about DHS initiatives, public safety, and other official activities. On September 16, 2010, the Department published a PIA on the Use of Social Networking Interactions and Applications (Communications/Outreach/Public Dialogue). Neither PIA is not intended to cover other social media activity such as monitoring initiatives, law enforcement and intelligence activities, and other similar operations. For more information on the Department's use of social media, visit www.dhs.gov/privacy.

SECTION 1.0. AUTHORITIES AND OTHER REQUIREMENTS

1.1. What Specific Legal Authorities and/or Agreements Permit and Define the Collection ofInformation by the Project in Question?

The President's Transparency and Open Government Memorandum14 (January 21, 2009) and the OMB Director's Open Government Directive Memorandum15 (December 8, 2009) directs federal departments and agencies to harness new technologies to engage the public and serve as one of the primary authorities motivating the Department's efforts to utilize unidirectional social media applications.

The Secretary of Homeland Security's Efficiency Review, 16 Section III, Office of Public Affairs Cross-Component Coordination Task Force Directive requires all Departmental unidirectional social media applications to be coordinated with OPA, unless otherwise directed by statute, executive order, or regulation.

When using those unidirectional social media applications listed in Appendix A, DHS is not permitted to actively seek PII. Because of the one-way nature of unidirectional social media applications, the Department will only receive PII if it is viewable through a public profile, if one exists.

Authorities supporting the Department's use of unidirectional social media applications include:

A. 6 U.S.C. § 112, "Secretary; functions;"
B. 6 U.S.C. § 142, "Privacy Officer;"
C. 5 U.S.C. § 301, the Federal Records Act;
D. 5 U.S.C. § 552a, the Privacy Act of 1974;
E. Section 208 of the E-Government Act of 2002;
F. The President's *Memorandum on Transparency and Open Government*, January 21, 2009;
G. *The OMB Director's Open Government Directive* Memorandum, December 8, 2009;
H. OMB Memorandum M-10-23, *Guidance for Agency Use of Third-Party Websites and Applications*, June 25, 2010;[17]
I. OMB Memorandum for the Heads of Executive Departments and Agencies, and Independent Regulatory Agencies, *Social Media, Web-Based Interactive Technologies, and the Paperwork Reduction Act*, April 7, 2010; [18]
J. The Secretary's Efficiency Review, Section III, Office of Public Affairs Cross-Component Coordination Task Force Directive;

As a result of this new technological relationship between the Department and the public, it is imperative that DHS engage the public in a manner that complies with federal accessibility, privacy, information technology security, and records laws. To ensure that the Department's use of unidirectional social media applications complies with federal laws, executive orders, regulations, and policies, and to apply standards consistently across the entire Department, the Office of the General Counsel (OGC), Office for Civil Rights and Civil Liberties (CRCL), Privacy Office (PRIV), Office of Public Affairs (OPA), Chief Information Security Office (CISO), and Office of Records Management (Records) will collaborate to ensure that all documents related to social media are cleared and to ensure that compliance issues are considered and coordinated before implementation.

1.2. What Privacy Act System of Records Notice(s) (SORN(s)) Apply to the Information?

When using the unidirectional social media applications listed in Appendix A, DHS is not permitted to actively seek PII. Because of the one-way nature of unidirectional social media applications, the Department will also not receive PII unless viewable through a public profile, if one exists. Therefore, no SORN is required.

1.3. Has a System Security Plan Been Completed for the Information System(S) Supporting the Project?

Unidirectional social media applications used by the Department for providing content may be external and operated by third-party entities. DHS may also develop its own widgets. However, the government may place content on these third party websites or applications. Therefore, no internal system security plan is currently required. Users of widgets used by DHS must consult the security policies of unidirectional social media applications they use for more information as applicable.

1.4. Does a Records Retention Schedule Approved by the National Archives and Records Administration (NARA) Exist?

The Department's Office of Records Management, Office of General Counsel, and other components are working together internally and with NARA to determine if the use of unidirectional social media applications creates records and if so the applicable records schedule(s). If it is determined that use of unidirectional social media applications creates government records, such records will be retained indefinitely until a records schedule is approved. Once a determination is made and an appropriate schedule identified and/or approved, the Department will follow that approved records schedule.

1.5. If the Information Is Covered by the Paperwork Reduction Act (PRA), Provide the OMB Control Number and the Agency Number for the Collection. If There Are Multiple Forms, Include a List in an Appendix

Whether or not the Department's use of unidirectional social media applications triggers the PRA is context dependent.[19] When using those unidirectional social media applications listed in Appendix A, DHS is not permitted to actively seek PII. Because of the one-way nature of unidirectional social media applications, the Department will also not receive PII unless viewable through a public profile, if one exists. Therefore, most uses of unidirectional social media applications will be exempt from the PRA. As part of the PIA review process, programs must determine whether or not the PRA will apply. Those programs that are subject to PRA may be required to conduct a separate PIA.

SECTION 2.0. CHARACTERIZATION OF THE INFORMATION

The following questions are intended to define the scope of the information requested and/or collected, as well as reasons for its collection.

2.1. Identify the Information the Project Collects, Uses, Disseminates, or Maintains

Consistent with DHS policy the Department may utilize unidirectional social media applications for external relations (communications and outreach) and to disseminate timely content to the public about DHS initiatives, public safety, and other official activities. DHS may use these unidirectional applications to inform the public on a range of topics including: 1) airport security processing; 2) access to and security at federal buildings; 3) man-made and natural disaster preparedness; 4) transportation security; 5) pandemic outbreaks; 6) border access and security; and 7) other public safety purposes.

DHS programs using unidirectional social media applications are not permitted to actively seek PII. Unidirectional social media applications may request PII at the time of registration based on individual requirements distinct from those of the Department. This collection will vary. The Department does not automatically have access to, and will not seek, the public's registration information, including PII, unless the information used during registration pre-populates a public profile, if one exists. Through use of non-interactive social media applications, DHS and public users may have an account and, by nature of the program, PII may transit and be displayed by the system during the signup/long-on transaction and subsequent interactions.

2.2. What Are the Sources of the Information and How Is the Information Collected for the Project?

Unidirectional social media applications may request PII at the time of registration based on individual requirements distinct from those of the Department. This collection will vary. Unless the information, including PII, used during registration pre-populates a public profile, if one exists, the Department does not automatically have access to, and will not seek, the public's registration information. Through use of non-interactive social media applications, DHS and public users may have an account and, by nature of the program, PII may transit and be displayed by the system during the sign-up/long-on transaction and subsequent interactions.

2.3. Does the Project Use Information from Commercial Sources or Publicly Available Data? If so, Explain Why and How this Information Is Used

DHS officials may disseminate content, one-way, to individuals and entities outside of the Department. Profiles, including PII, are used by these unidirectional social media applications and may be searchable by an individual's information. This functionality allows users to share content with others on a web-based platform provided by the host. Unidirectional social media applications may, among other uses, also employ user-defined data to advertise products.

2.4. Discuss How Accuracy of the Data Is Ensured

DHS is not actively collecting PII. It is disseminating public content related to its mission. When DHS uses unidirectional social media applications to disseminate content outside of the Department, it will work to ensure accuracy of content it disseminates.

2.5. Privacy Impact Analysis: Related to Characterization of the Information

Risk: Given the nature of unidirectional social media applications, PII may transit and be displayed by the system during the sign-up/long-on transaction as well as being published on a public profile, if one exists.

Mitigation: To mitigate this risk, DHS has trained its staff not to actively collect PII or to enter it into the Department's systems.

SECTION 3.0. USES OF THE INFORMATION

The following questions require a clear description of the project's use of information.

3.1. Describe How and Why the Project Uses the Information

The Department may utilize certain unidirectional social media applications for external relations (communications and outreach) and to disseminate timely content to the public about DHS initiatives, public safety, and other official activities. When using those unidirectional social media applications listed in Appendix A, DHS is not permitted to actively seek PII. The Department will only have access to PII when it is viewable through a public profile, if one exists.

3.2. Does the Project Use Technology to Conduct Electronic Searches, Queries, or Analyses in an Electronic Database to Discover or Locate a Predictive Pattern or an Anomaly? If so, State How DHS Plans to Use Such Results

The Department will not dictate what technology the unidirectional social media applications use to analyze their products. The Department will not produce data except, potentially, in instances where the Department seeks to better understand the breadth and reach of mission-related content it is sharing through unidirectional social media applications, however, the analysis will only attempt to understand the breadth and reach through aggregated data. The Department will not identify an individual user.

3.3. Are There Other Components with Assigned Roles and Responsibilities within the System?

Unless otherwise directed by statute, executive order, or regulation the Department's public affairs officials will serve as the primary account holders for all unidirectional social media applications hosted on third party sites across the Department and will manage and approve all DHS content disseminated through these public-facing applications. The Department's public affairs officials will ensure that all disseminated content falls within the appropriate requirements for publicly available content. OPA will, when necessary, act as the final authority on what content is acceptable for posting.

3.4. Privacy Impact Analysis: Related to the Uses of Information

Risk: Given the nature of unidirectional social media applications, PII may transit and be displayed by the system during the sign-up/long-on transaction as well as being published on a public profile, if one exists. The dissemination of content and the viewing of a user's public profile, if one exists, may expose Department users to PII and that information may be inappropriately incorporated into Departmental files.

Mitigation: To mitigate this risk, the Department recommends public users limit the PII submitted to unidirectional social media applications and made available on their profile, if one exists, viewable to the outside. DHS is not permitted to actively seek PII.

SECTION 4.0. NOTICE

The following questions seek information about the project's notice to the individual about the information collected, the right to consent to uses of said information, and the right to decline to provide information.

4.1. How Does the Project Provide Individuals Notice Prior to the Collection of Information? If Notice Is Not Provided, Explain Why Not

The Department shall set-up official accounts on third party applications and service providers which clearly establish that the accounts are managed by DHS. DHS may also develop its own widgets. For example, the Department shall use the DHS seal on the unidirectional social media applications when technologically possible. In addition, employees responsible for managing such applications should clearly identify themselves, such as "DHS John Q. Employee," when disseminating to the public. The Department's public affairs officials are content approvers for the Department.

In advance of utilizing unidirectional social media applications, the Department will examine the privacy policy, if one is available, of the application to evaluate the risks to determine whether it is appropriate for the Department's use. Additionally, to the extent feasible, the Department will post a privacy notice on the application itself. When posting a link that leads to an application, the agency will provide an alert to the visitor, such as a statement adjacent to the link or a "pop-up." The statement or "pop up" will explain that visitors are being directed to a nongovernment website, which may have different privacy policies from those of the Department's official application. Users should also consult the privacy policies of unidirectional social media applications they subscribe to for more information as they apply. The Department's privacy policy can be viewed at http://www.dhs.gov/xutil/gc_1157139158971.shtm.

4.2. What Opportunities Are Available for Individuals to Consent to Uses, Decline to Provide Information, or Opt out of the Project?

In advance of utilizing unidirectional social media applications, the Department will examine the privacy policy, if one is available, of the application to evaluate the risks to determine whether it is appropriate for the Department's use. Additionally, to the extent feasible, the Department will post a privacy notice on the application itself. When posting a link that leads to an application, the agency will provide an alert to the visitor, such as a statement adjacent to the link or a "pop-up." The statement or "pop up" will explain that visitors are being directed to a nongovernment website, which may have different privacy policies from those of the Department's official application. Users should also consult the privacy policies of unidirectional social media applications they subscribe to for more information as they apply. The Department's privacy policy can be viewed at http://www.dhs.gov/xutil/ gc_1157139158971.shtm.

As the PII collected by the unidirectional social media application is submitted for registration voluntarily by individuals to populate a public profile, if one exists, the Department cannot provide an opportunity to decline to provide information. With regard to the rights users may have on the unidirectional social media application, individuals should consult the privacy policies of the applications they subscribe to for more information.

4.3. Privacy Impact Analysis: Related to Notice

Risk: There is a risk that public users will not know who they are receiving content from when sent by the Department and whether the account is official or fictitious.

Mitigation: The Department shall set-up official accounts that clearly establish that the accounts are managed by DHS. For example, the Department shall use the DHS seal on the unidirectional social media applications when technologically possible. In addition, employees responsible for managing such applications should clearly identify themselves, such as "DHS John Q. Employee," when communicating with the public. The Department's public affairs officials are content approvers for the Department. In addition, the Department will work with third party providers to remove any non-DHS accounts that imply that they are official.

Risk: There is a risk that public users will not understand that the unidirectional social media tools may be third party owned and that the privacy policies belong to the third party.

Mitigation: In advance of utilizing a unidirectional social media application, the Department will examine the privacy policy, if one is available, to evaluate the risks to determine whether it is appropriate for the Department's use. Additionally, to the extent feasible, the Department will post a privacy notice on the unidirectional social media application itself. Users should also consult the privacy policies of unidirectional social media applications they subscribe to for more information as they apply. The Department's privacy policy can be viewed at http://www.dhs.gov/xutil/gc_1157139158971.shtm .

SECTION 5.0. DATA RETENTION BY THE PROJECT

The following questions are intended to outline how long the project retains the information after the initial collection.

5.1. Explain How Long and for What Reason the Information Is Retained

When using those unidirectional social media applications listed in Appendix A, DHS is not permitted to actively seek PII. Because of the one-way nature of unidirectional social media applications, the Department will also not receive PII unless viewable through a public profile, if one exists.

The Department's Office of Records Management, Office of General Counsel, and other components are working internally, as well as with the NARA, to determine the records schedule. Until the records schedule is approved, records are maintained indefinitely. Once approved, the Department will follow that approved records schedule.

Records may also be maintained by the unidirectional social media applications. Check specific unidirectional social media applications for details on records retention.

5.2. Privacy Impact Analysis: Related to Retention

Risk: Retaining content for longer than is relevant and necessary can introduce privacy risks such as unauthorized use and disclosure.

Mitigation: To mitigate this risk, the Department will only maintain the mission-related content it sends via unidirectional social media applications. The Department's Office of Records Management, Office of General Counsel, and other components are working internally, as well as with the National Archives and Records Administration, to determine the records schedule. Once approved, the Department will follow that approved records schedule.

SECTION 6.0. INFORMATION SHARING

The following questions are intended to describe the scope of the project information sharing external to the Department. External sharing encompasses sharing with other federal, state and local government, and private sector entities.

6.1. Is Information Shared outside of DHS as Part of the Normal Agency Operations? If so, Identify the Organization(S) and How the Information Is Accessed and How It Is to Be Used

The mission-related content sent via unidirectional social media applications will be available to any and all users on a unidirectional social media application who are able to access the public-facing side of an account. The Department will only disseminate content after it has been appropriately approved and vetted by the Department's public affairs officials. In addition, all content will be posted on a Department website.

6.2. Describe How the External Sharing Noted in 6.1 Is Compatible with the SORN Noted in 1.2

The mission-related content sent via unidirectional social media applications will be available to any and all users on a unidirectional social media application who are able to access the public-facing side of an account.

The Department will only disseminate content after it has been appropriately approved and vetted by the Department's public affairs officials.

When using those unidirectional social media applications listed in Appendix A, DHS is not permitted to actively seek PII. Because of the one-way nature of unidirectional social media applications, the Department will also not receive PII unless viewable through a public profile, if one exists. Therefore, no SORN is required.

6.3. Does the Project Place Limitations on Re-Dissemination?

When using those unidirectional social media applications listed in Appendix A, DHS is not permitted to actively seek PII. Because of the one-way nature of unidirectional social media applications, the Department will also not receive PII unless viewable through a public profile, if one exists. Therefore, no re-dissemination will occur.

6.4. Describe How the Project Maintains a Record of any Disclosures Outside of the Department

Content sent via the Department's unidirectional social media application is publicly available therefore it will be accessible to anyone with an internet connection. Content may also be shared by other electronic means and in paper form. In doing so, the Department's existing policies and procedures for information sharing govern.[20] The Department's public affairs officials are content approvers for the Department. This includes sharing of mission-related content outside of the Department.

Because of the one-way nature of unidirectional social media applications, the Department will also not receive PII unless viewable through a public profile, if one exists. Therefore, no PII will be disclosed outside the Department.

6.5. Privacy Impact Analysis: Related to Information Sharing

Risk: Sharing too much mission-related content is a risk inherent in this process. This has the potential of exposing the Department to more public user profiles.

Mitigation: Department employees share only as much content as necessary in the performance of official Department duties with those who have a need-to-know. The Department's employees and contractors will be trained on the appropriate use and sharing of unidirectional social media application content.

Because of the one-way nature of unidirectional social media applications, the Department will also not receive PII unless viewable through a public profile, if one exists. Therefore, no PII will be disclosed outside the Department.

SECTION 7.0 REDRESS

The following questions seek information about processes in place for individuals to seek redress which may include access to records about themselves, ensuring the accuracy of the information collected about them, and/or filing complaints.

7.1. What Are the Procedures that Allow Individuals to Access Their Information?

As a general matter, the Department is not collecting PII on individuals and so there is no PII that an individual could redress. Nevertheless, the Department's public affairs officials will post their contact information on the unidirectional social media applications to allow any individual to contact the Department. Individuals should also consult the privacy policies of the unidirectional social media applications they subscribe to for more information related to those unidirectional social media applications access provisions.

7.2. What Procedures Are in Place to Allow the Subject Individual to Correct Inaccurate or Erroneous Information?

As noted above, the Department is not collecting PII about individuals therefore generally will not have a record that needs to be corrected. In most instances the individual is able to correct the public profile, if one exists, on the unidirectional social media application directly. The Department's public affairs officials will post their contact information on the application to allow any individual to contact the Department. Individuals should also consult the privacy policies of the applications they subscribe to for more information related to those unidirectional social media applications access provisions. The Department's privacy policy can be viewed at http://www.dhs.gov/xutil/gc_ 1157139158971.shtm.

7.3. How Does the Project Notify Individuals About the Procedures for Correcting Their Information?

As noted above, the Department's dissemination of content via unidirectional social media applications does not include collecting information about individuals therefore generally will not have a record held by the Department that needs to be corrected. If the individual subscribes to a widget where the owner of the widget requires the individual to register before accessing the application, in most instances the individual is able to correct PII on the unidirectional social media application directly.

The Department's public affairs officials will post their contact information on the application to allow any individual to contact the Department. Individuals should also consult the privacy policies of the applications they subscribe to for more information related to those unidirectional social media applications access provisions. The Department's privacy policy can be viewed at http://www.dhs.gov/xutil/gc_1157139158971 .shtm.

7.4. Privacy Impact Analysis: Related to Redress

For activities under this PIA, the Department will not be collecting PII. In most instances the unidirectional social media application is designed so that the individual has direct control over his/her PII and can make any corrections required. Nevertheless, the Department's public affairs officials will post their contact information on the applications to allow any individual to contact the Department. This contact information, in most cases, will be in the form of standard email and physical mailing addresses.

The public user profile PII available on unidirectional social media applications, if one exists, is largely user-generated, meaning the individual chooses the amount of information available about himself or herself as well as the ease with which it can be accessed by other users. Thus, the primary account holder should be able to redress any concerns through the unidirectional social media application. Individuals should also consult the privacy policies of the unidirectional social media applications they subscribe to for more information related to those non-interactive social media applications access provisions. The Department's privacy policy can be viewed at http://www.dhs.gov/xutil/gc_1157139158971.shtm.

SECTION 8.0. AUDITING AND ACCOUNTABILITY

The following questions are intended to describe technical and policy based safeguards and security measures.

The unidirectional social media applications listed in Appendix A are subject to Privacy Compliance Reviews by the DHS Privacy Office.

8.2. Describe What Privacy Training Is Provided to Users Either Generally or Specifically Relevant to the Project

The Department's federal employees and contractors are provided annual privacy training. Officials approving, disseminating, and sharing mission-related content are provided additional training by the Department's public affairs officials.

8.3. What Procedures Are in Place to Determine which Users May Access the Information and How Does the Project Determine Who Has Access?

Where the Department uses unidirectional social media applications for content distribution it will establish official accounts which will be controlled by the Department's public affairs officials who will ensure that only authorized individuals have access. DHS must set-up an official account which clearly establishes that the account is managed by DHS. For example, components should use the DHS seal on the unidirectional social media application when technologically possible. In addition, employees responsible for managing such applications should clearly identify themselves, such as "DHS John Q. Employee," when interacting with the public.

As part of their official contractual duties, when supervised by a federal employee, contractors may provide support for to the Department's unidirectional social media applications.

8.4. How Does the Project Review and Approve Information Sharing Agreements, Mous, New Uses of the Information, New Access to the System by Organizations within DHS and Outside?

As a result of this new technological relationship between the Department and the public, it is imperative that DHS engage the public in a manner that complies with federal accessibility, privacy, information technology security, and records laws. To ensure that the Department's use of social media complies with federal laws, executive orders, regulations, and policies, and to apply standards consistently across the entire Department, the offices of OGC, CRCL, PRIV, OPA, CISO, and Records will collaborate to ensure that all documents related to unidirectional social media applications are cleared to ensure compliance issues are considered and coordinated before implementation.

Appendix A of this PIA will serve as a listing, to be updated periodically, of DHS unidirectional social media applications, approved by the Chief Privacy Officer, that follow the requirements and analytical understanding outlined in this PIA.

APPENDIX A

Non-interactive social media applications covered by this PIA include:

DHS Office of Public Affairs

Google Calendar – April 1, 2011
RestoretheGulf.gov – April 1, 2011

FEMA
Online News Room – March 14, 2011

Widgets – March 14, 2011

Smartphone App – August 8, 2011

End Notes

[1] Other names for these applications include, but are not limited to: portlets, gadgets, plasmoids and screenlets. The function specified in the Abstract, rather than the name of a particular vendor or platform uses, serves to specify what a "widget" is.

[2] Applications that can function on any site that accepts external content, including social networks, blog platforms, start pages, desktop platforms, or personal website pages. Widgets can be built to function differently on each platform, delivering varying degrees of integration with a social network, from accessing and using social media data to not interacting with the platform at all.

[3] Same as footnote 2 but received and viewed on a mobile device.

[4] A series of digital media files, either audio or video, that are downloaded directly or are streamed webcasting.

[5] Audio or video files that can begin playing as they are being downloaded.

[6] Text communication service component of phone, web or mobile communication systems, using standardized communications protocols that allow the exchange of short text messages.

[7] A web-content format that alerts users to new content on a website. They enable users to avoid the conventional methods of browsing or searching for information on websites. RSS feeds may be deployed as widgets or as standalone applications in web-browsers or other software.

[8] If a component of the Department has an operational need to use unidirectional social media applications that is outside the scope of the requirements and analytical understanding outlined in this PIA, a separate PIA must be written for that component's use of unidirectional social media applications to address the specific privacy concerns that are unique to that initiative for consideration by the Chief Privacy Officer.

[9] President Barack Obama, Memorandum on *Transparency and Open Government* (January 21, 2009), *available at* http://www.gpoaccess.gov/presdocs/2009/DCPD200900010.pdf.

[10] OMB Memorandum M-10-06, *Open Government Directive* (December 8, 2009), *available at* http://www.whitehouse.gov/omb/assets/memoranda_2010/m10-06.pdf.

[11] A type of user interface that allows users to interact with programs in more ways than just computers such as: hand-held devices such as MP3 players, portable media players or gaming devices; household appliances and office equipment with images rather than text commands. A GUI offers graphical icons, and visual indicators, as opposed to text-based interfaces, typed command labels or text navigation to fully represent the information and actions available to a user.

[12] OMB Memorandum M-10-23, *Guidance for Agency Use of Third-Party Websites and Applications* (June 25, 2010), *available at* http://www.whitehouse.gov/omb/ assets/ memoranda_2010/m10-23.pdf.

[13] The Secretary's Efficiency Review, Section III, Office of Public Affairs Cross-Component Coordination Task Force Directive *available at* http://dhsconnect.dhs.gov/policies/EfficiencyReviewMaterials/90_ER_-_DHS_Communications_-final_guidance_intranet.pdf.

[14] President Barack Obama, Memorandum on *Transparency and Open Government* (January 21, 2009), *available at* http://www.gpoaccess.gov/presdocs/2009/DCPD200900010.pdf.

[15] OMB Memorandum M-10-06, *Open Government Directive* (December 8, 2009), *available at* http://www.whitehouse.gov/omb/assets/memoranda_2010/m10-06.pdf.

[16] The Secretary's Efficiency Review, Section III, Office of Public Affairs Cross-Component Coordination Task Force Directive *available at* http://dhsconnect.dhs.gov/policies/ Efficiency Review Materials/90_ER_-_DHS_ Communications_-final_guidance_intranet .pdf.

[17] OMB Memorandum M-10-23, *Guidance for Agency Use of Third-Party Websites and Applications* (June 25, 2010), *available at* http://www.whitehouse.gov/omb/assets/ memoranda_2010/m10-23.pdf.

[18] OMB Memorandum for the Heads of Executive Departments and Agencies, and Independent Regulatory Agencies, *Social Media, Web-Based Interactive Technologies, and the Paperwork Reduction Act (*April 7, 2010), *available at* http://www.whitehouse.gov/ sites/default/files/omb/assets/inforeg/PRA_Gen_ICRs_5-28-2010.pdf.

[19] OMB Memorandum for the Heads of Executive Departments and Agencies, and Independent Regulatory Agencies, *Social Media, Web-Based Interactive Technologies, and the Paperwork Reduction Act (*April 7, 2010), *available at* http://www.whitehouse.gov/sites/ default/files/omb/assets/inforeg/PRA_Gen_ICRs_5-28-2010.pdf.

INDEX